Note. [illegible]
roo[illegible]
Lile[illegible]
both worked with Jane
Hirshfield in workshop

MW00592739

# THE MARRAM GRASS

Rocks at beach east of Monk's Head

# THE MARRAM GRASS

## Poetry & Otherness

*Anne Simpson*

GASPEREAU PRESS LIMITED
*Printers & Publishers*
2009

sanddollars

*In memory of two generous spirits:*
*George S. Sanderson and*
*John Arther Murphy*

Wild
applis

# *A Hundred and Fifty Psalms at Twilight*

I look out the window: a hundred and fifty
psalms pass through the twilight . . .

YEHUDA AMICHAI[1]

Most days I walk with my two dogs on the Fairmont Trail, off the Harbour Road, in Antigonish County, through a tract of land that is sometimes whiskered and tipped with the first frost, or densely overgrown and haloed with the black flies of summer, or extravagantly wet and muddy, every leaf running with water. Occasionally I catch glimpses of snowshoe hares and grouse; once I encountered a black bear that had been feasting on wild apples (it looked at me quizzically, and I backed away as a person would do for royalty, calling for the dogs—no, yelling for the dogs to follow).

I saw the bear in October, but months before, in late May, I was hiking farther up the trail, on the Fairmont Ridge. Passing through a cathedral of old hemlocks, I recalled being told some of them were well over two hundred years old. Sun slant, pockets of charcoal-coloured shadow. Bunchberries and ostrich ferns. The hemlocks stand on a slope that remains dark and cool even in the heat of July and

1 Yehuda Amichai, "Summer Evening by the Window with Psalms," trans. Robert Alter, *The New Yorker* (New York: Condé Nast Publications, July 28, 2008), vol. LXXXIV, no. 22, 74.

August. That morning a barred owl was roosting in a tree, perhaps a maple; when it heard me, it took flight. There was a commotion as it left the branch, but no sound as it flew, flecked wings—with their characteristic pattern of bars—outspread. When it settled, it looked at me. I looked at it. Its jet-coloured eyes, forward-facing, were held by sclerotic rings that allowed it to stare fixedly ahead, gripping me as if I were prey.

I have an ink-brush drawing of an owl hanging on the wall in my office, a gift from Linda Johns, an artist and writer who lives not far from Antigonish. The owl in the drawing has exactly such a penetrating gaze. As delicately rendered as lacework, its face is superimposed over a dead tree trunk, gnarled branches stretching up to the night sky. Above, there is a full moon, which is about the size of one of the owl's eyes. When I saw the barred owl at Fairmont, I was reminded of the ink-brush drawing. To be held by such a gaze is to be held immobile, as if the gaze suggests that one is known, entirely and completely known. The barred owl is one of the few owls whose eyes are not ringed with yellow; instead, they are entirely dark, and perhaps all the more compelling. Are we known, I wondered, by the things that see us? Do we reciprocate, by attempting to know what we see?

⊰•⊱

When we sense the wild around us, we're immediately aware of its gestures. In his poem "From March '79,"

Tomas Tranströmer reveals how the land speaks to us, how it addresses us:

> Tired of all who come with words, words but no language
> I went to the snow-covered island.
> The wild does not have words.
> The unwritten pages spread themselves out in all directions.
> I come across the marks of roe-deer's hooves in the snow.
>
> Language, but no words.[2]

Out of the hush of this snow-covered island, Tranströmer is committed to shape the quiet into a form we understand, even as he might resist putting it into words.

We inhabit language bodily, letting the air move through us, allowing ourselves to be thresholds. Yet a sense of otherness, which might speak through us, is too often scoured away. We favour the analytical model; we depend upon it. There is nothing wrong with it, but we have allowed it to supersede other forms of expression: astonishment is ironed out of it, lament and ecstasy eradicated. The language we have come to value is utilitarian. It has clarity. It has purpose. It provides us with a means to an end. We place a premium on language that gets the job done quickly and efficiently—a mere tool employed by active people. But in considering it simply as something useful, we may have gradually erased the ways of knowing that are of the body and sundered the connections we have to all that is around

---

**2** Tomas Tranströmer, *Selected Poems, 1954–1986,* trans. John F. Deane, ed. Robert Hass (New York: The Ecco Press, 1987), 159.

us. The very fabric of our thinking has been torn away, frayed from the land, from the wild.

In order to talk about the wild, we may need another way of speaking, or of writing, since there is more than one way to know the world, more than one way to express it. Or perhaps we simply need to expand our notion of language. But what would it be like, this enriched language? It would have an intimate connection with the body and the space inhabited by the body. It would embrace multiplicity. It would allow for, as Gary Snyder says, "the common coexistence of levels, codes, slangs, dialects, whole languages and languages even of different families—in one speaker."[3] Snyder goes on to say that we need to look beyond the human, though, and the dialogue that we need to consider "would be among all beings, toward a rhetoric of ecological relationships."[4] It is possible to envision the interaction between human and other-than-human as an interpenetration of worlds, one that thrums with the slangs and dialects of the wild. Such a language is a richly textured tapestry of speech, a caterwauling of sounds.

It stands as an invitation. For what? Surely it's an invitation for something unfamiliar, mapping the arc of desire. A way of bending close to listen. In his essay "The Intertwining—The Chiasm," Maurice Merleau-Ponty observes that "our existence as sonorous beings for others and for ourselves contain(s) everything required for there to be speech

---

**3** Gary Snyder, *The Practice of the Wild: Essays* (New York: North Point Press, 1990), 72. **4** Ibid, 68.

from the one to the other, speech about the world. And, in a sense, to understand a phrase is nothing else than to fully welcome it in its sonorous being, or, as we put it so well, to *hear what it says* [*l'entendre*]."[5] To welcome such language, then, is to bring it into ourselves, to listen to it.

But we tend to see ourselves lending language to the world, rather than discovering what is constantly being offered to us. We often ignore the complex communication of all that surrounds us: a ruffed grouse, disturbed, taking flight in almost comical frenzy, an uprooted hemlock crashing to the earth, a pagoda of white blossoms poised on an elderberry bush, making the faintest sound as it is blown in a breeze. Wild speech is thick with rustling, barking, whirring. A feathered sort of talk, a language furred with moss, netted with lichen. Perhaps it is beyond us to hear it, to note it, or be able, in any sense, to suggest its cawings and clamourings. If we were able to convey it, surely it would be overgrown and tangled, dripping with muck, or traced with pollen. When we make the attempt to write of the wild, Edward Casey asks us to consider it wholly, since "it is not so much the direct object of sight or thought or recollection as what we feel *with* and *around*, *under* and *above*, *before* and *behind*."[6] It could be understood as another skin, enveloping us. Or put another way, human skin could be that which

**5** Maurice Merleau-Ponty, "The Intertwining—The Chiasm," in *The Merleau-Ponty Reader*, eds. Ted Toadvine and Leonard Lawlor (Evanston, IL: Northwestern University Press, 2007), 413. **6** Edward S. Casey, *Getting Back into Place: Toward a Renewed Understanding of the Place-World* (Bloomington, IN: Indiana University Press, 1993), 313.

touches the skin of the world: one thing next to another. Touched and touching.

⋆

The barred owl has various names. *Strix varia* is its Latin name, but it is also known as the eight hooter, the rain owl, the wood owl, the striped owl, and the hoot owl: this last one is the name by which it is best known. I'd heard it, in fact, a week before, and thought to myself that I was, indeed, listening to the call of an owl. No—it couldn't be. I stopped. I wasn't certain it was an owl's hooting, not being well versed in the birder's art. But the call was distinctive, coming in quick, quizzical whoops that ran along in a string of aspirated sounds, hence its name: eight hooter. I thought about how the hoots increased in intensity, progressively building to full throttle at the end: *whoo, whoo, whoo, whoo, whoo, whoo, whoo, whoo-OO-oo.* I realized that I heard it in exactly the same way I listen to a line of poetry; without even knowing I was doing it, I counted beats, trying to catch its particular rhythm.

Once, while I was walking in another part of the Fairmont with Peter Jackson, who designed the trails he subsequently built on this land, we heard a peculiar song. The bird—not a thrush, not a warbler—that made this cheery call sounded like a trapeze artist who had slid off the high wire to splash, spluttering, in a pool of water below. There was a quality of jazz riff and knee-slapping laughter to it: a combination of tomfoolery and artistry. A crazy ecstasy.

Its intonations made sense to both of us. It was

sophisticated, playful, and other-than-human; it delighted us. I was reminded of being in Italy years before, as a student involved in a program run by the Ontario College of Art and Design, and understanding, for the first time, a joke in a language that was not my own. I was at a party at someone's home in the hilly Tuscan countryside, in a village called Passo dei Pecorai, and the gathering was a boisterous event. The family was not wealthy, but the tables were laden: everyone was commanded to eat, and keep eating, until the feast was reduced to scraps on the platters. There was quick banter back and forth between old friends. Someone told a joke I didn't understand, and a friend next to me repeated it, slowly. For a moment, I sensed a hinge between languages as a door swung open.

The carnival sound of the unknown bird's song intrigued me, because, once again, I sensed the door of language swinging open. Afterwards, I listened, several times, to a compact disc that catalogued the calls and songs of 267 species of birds of eastern North America.[7] By the end, I felt as though I'd listened to a quirky, talented group of 267 musicians playing a motley assortment of instruments though it wasn't the same as hearing the overlapping of the myriad songs outside. I recognized the hoots of the barred owl, although I couldn't identify the call of the unknown bird. Perhaps it was a northern mockingbird, but it remained a mystery, a song that lay on the cusp of language. Still, I could almost hear what Thoreau called the "mother-wit" of

---

**7** Cornell Laboratory of Ornithology, Interactive Audio, *A Field Guide to Bird Songs: Eastern / Central Bird Songs*, 3rd Edition, The Peterson Field Guide Series (New York: Houghton Mifflin Co., 1990).

nature, a kind of wild language, based on wild intelligence: "The Spaniards have a good term to express this wild and dusky knowledge, *Grammatica parda*, tawny grammar ..."[8]

Thoreau doesn't go on to say much else about it, but tawny grammar, I think, would include beak and claw. It would be many-voiced, as if numerous strands of sound ran through it at once. But how else might it be described? Most likely it would be ever-changing, ever-fluctuating; it wouldn't be fixed or closed. Because of its openness, it would be innovative and experimental, shifting and renewing its protean forms; it would work in all manner of roundabout ways, inquiring, speaking, shouting, begging, singing, berating, murmuring, coaxing—and calling out. It would sound like poetry.

---

I imagine tawny grammar to be different from, but connected to, the quotidian grammar we all employ: the use of one would not mean doing away with the other. Recently, I asked a friend to imagine a world without grammar. He couldn't. I couldn't either. Grammar allows us the roads, streets, stop signs, and traffic lights of language. It is a lawful system: the one by which we abide. If we are good citizens, we drive along Main Street at the proper speed, and make a signal when turning onto Church.

I flipped through a grammar book that I once used as

---

**8** Henry David Thoreau, "Walking," in *Great Short Works of Henry David Thoreau,* ed. Wendell Glick (*The Atlantic Monthly,* 1862, rpt. New York: Perennial Classics, 1982), 319.

a teacher of English as a Second Language (*Basic English Grammar*) just to remind myself of the point at which someone might begin the teaching of English—ah, yes, a lesson on the verb "to be." Perhaps it is entirely natural that English language learning should begin in this realm, with our own existence front and centre as we sense things through the tips of our fingers, through our mouths, through our eyes. The verb "to be" acts as an auxiliary, a bridge to connect other verbs: "I am eating some blueberries." We're always doing something—eating, sleeping, walking, working—beyond merely existing. But we are obsessed with the fact of *being*. The teaching of grammar begins with the self and then it expands. If we are unsure about ourselves and our place in the scheme of things, all we need to do is learn another language. A first conversation might run something like this: "What is your name? My name is Mizuki. Where are you from? I am from Japan. What do you do? I am an oceanographer."

Our fascination with ontology is built into language. But problems arise in language, Nietzsche says, because of our belief in the self. He goes on to point out how philosophy makes claims about reason based on claims about the self: "Everywhere [reason] sees a doer and doing; it believes in the will as *the* cause; it believes in the ego, in the ego as being, in the ego as substance, and it projects this faith in the ego-substance upon all things—only thereby does it first *create* the concept of a 'thing.'"[9] Nietzsche's comments are

---

**9** Friedrich Nietzsche, *Twilight of the Idols* in *The Portable Nietzsche*, ed. and trans. Walter Kaufmann (1954, rpt. New York: Viking Penguin, 1982), 483.

part of a larger critique of the assumptions about reason. His irritation is concentrated on Descartes, whose ladder of reason was braced by *cogito ergo sum,* the rungs of which ascended to God—*causa sui*. For Nietzsche, both God and grammar are Cartesian concepts: "I am afraid we are not rid of God because we still have faith in grammar."[10] Nietzsche was an iconoclast; he wanted to poke holes in the privileged discourse. What he demonstrates is that grammar is simply a system of order, one in which we have faith.

The phenomenologist Martin Heidegger, whose life overlapped Nietzsche's by a few years at the end of the nineteenth century, was deeply interested in the relationship between being and language. He puts it this way: "Language is the house of Being. In its home man dwells. Those who think and those who create with words are the guardians of this home."[11] We dwell within language as we dwell inside being, the home we possess. However, for Heidegger, says Richard Rorty, "history is a sequence of 'words of Being'—the words of the great philosophers who gave successive historical epochs their self-image, and thereby built successive 'houses of Being.' The history of the West, which Heidegger also called the history of Being, is a narrative of the changes in human beings' image of themselves, their sense of what ultimately matters."[12] In other words, Rorty implies, Western philosophy was all about the self. It isn't a surprise, then, that language is self-centred.

---

**10** Ibid, 483. **11** Martin Heidegger, *Letter on Humanism* in *Basic Writings,* ed. David Farrell Krell (English trans. 1977, rpt. New York: Harper Collins, 1993), 217. **12** Richard Rorty, "A Master from Germany: One of the Greatest Western Philosophers was also a Nazi" (*New York Times Books On the Web,* May 3, 1998).

But if language is the house of being, this house has the potential to become a crematorium. For Paul Celan (born Paul Antschel) a Romanian Jew who lost his parents in the Holocaust, language remained intact after the Second World War, but it was seared by that passage. In a speech upon his acceptance of the Bremen Prize for German Literature in 1958, Celan, recalling the war, observed:

> Only one thing remained reachable, close and secure amid all losses: language. Yes, language. In spite of everything, it remained secure against loss. But it had to go through its own lack of answers, through terrifying silence, through the thousand darknesses of murderous speech. It went through. It gave me no words for what was happening, but went through it. Went through and could resurface, 'enriched' by it all.[13]

Heidegger, too, continued to think about language. While the self appears to be at the centre of language-making in his *Letter on Humanism* (first published in France in 1947), his thinking was shifting, and more than twenty years later, in an essay called "Language," he seems to have begun thinking of language in somewhat different terms: "To reflect on language … demands that we enter into the speaking of language in order to take up our stay with language, i.e., within *its* speaking, not within our own."[14] Still, even if language speaks, he is careful to examine this idea further in order to unravel it. Humans are the ones doing the speaking. And

---

**13** Paul Celan, "Speech on the Occasion of Receiving the Literature Prize of the Free Hanseatic City of Bremen," in Celan's *Collected Prose*, trans. Rosmarie Waldrop (Riverdale-on-Hudson, NY: The Sheep Meadow Press, 1986), 34. **14** Martin Heidegger, "Language," in *Poetry, Language, Thought*, trans. Albert Hofstadter (1971, rpt. New York: Harper & Row, 1975), 190.

so, as he says, "Hence we cannot say 'Language speaks'. For this would be to say: 'It is language that first brings man about, brings him into existence'."[15]

So—we exist; we speak. We are not spoken into the world by language. But towards the end of this essay, Heidegger seems to shift ground. Now "Language speaks. Man speaks in that he responds to language. Its speaking speaks for us in what has been spoken."[16] Language takes on a creative, generative role, bringing humans into the sphere of speaking. It is as if language, as a larger, all-embracing consciousness or Being, calls us into consciousness. When we respond to the call of language, we don't seem to speak to one another but to the entity that is language. We may have been sealed off from otherness. As well, language, as Heidegger would have it, has a special, pure form—that of poetry.

⥪•⥭

Poetry *does* operate differently than ordinary language, but one wonders if that makes it purer. Isn't it simply a different way of approaching things? If so, what does poetry include, or dispense with, in terms of its approach? To think about this a bit further, I began the experiment of imagining a world without grammar (though I don't find this easy to do; I want to stick to the rules of the road instead). We might manage without grammar, but language would be disjointed. We'd have fragments instead of complete

---

**15** Ibid, 192. **16** Ibid, 210.

sentences, something like this: Wind. Rain. The sound of tree branches, cracking.

In a world without grammar, consequences would not follow from causes in the hierarchical structure we know so well. Words linking ideas in time, as well as showing relationships in terms of cause and effect, wouldn't be available to us. We wouldn't be able to show how one event influenced another event, since we wouldn't have the language to gather and synthesize ideas. We wouldn't be able to reason. Such a language might give us discrete units of thought, in sentence form, but these could slip into run-on sentences that might, or might not, come to an end. Punctuation marks, like the comma, colon, semi-colon, and period, would be discarded. Language might leap or gallop, or it might be arrested in mid-flight—

And it would not give us history: tales gathered together into larger stories of nations. It would not reveal beginnings and endings because it would have no use for them. What we would have, then, would be language outside memory, outside history, outside time. And, ultimately, it would become a blizzard of scatterings. We would stand between language and silence, like the speaker in "The Snow Man" by Wallace Stevens:

> the listener, who listens in the snow,
> And, nothing himself, beholds
> Nothing that is not there and the nothing that is.[17]

---

**17** Wallace Stevens, "The Snow Man," in *The Palm at the End of the Mind: Selected Poems and a Play,* ed. Holly Stevens (New York: Vintage Books, 1972), 54.

So while at one end of the scale we have language as an apparently ordered system, albeit one in which we have faith, at the other end we have language beginning its descent into incoherence. Poetry exists somewhere between order and chaos, thriving on both: sometimes providing an orderly sequence, sometimes giving us mere flutterings of thought blown around the page. It isn't pure; if anything, it's impure and messy. But it does, occasionally, make the attempt to move to the farthest edge of the linguistic, where it plays at the border of silence. (No wonder people always want poetry to be accessible: this need for accessibility is a desire to shake sense into a wily creature, one that is always trying to free itself from constraints.)

It is often by means of bits and pieces, rather than the paraphernalia of complete sentences, that poetry works most effectively. Its concurrent interest in the evanescent and the timeless—or instant and era, simultaneously—is not overly concerned with events on a large scale, as in reportage, or even on a small scale, as in diaries or journals.

Slicing through time, it grasps the significance of laden moments, intensifying them with emotional nuance, and revealing them as if caught inside amber. Poetry may or may not make a case, give evidence, or come to conclusions, though it does not set reason—or grammar—aside. Yet the point that it makes may be lightning-sharp and elegantly simple, as in the first stanza of a poem by Emily Dickinson:

> It was not death, for I stood up,
> And all the dead lie down;

> It was not night, for all the bells
> Put out their tongues, for noon.[18]

Without disclosing the cogs and wheels of its workings, poetry can give us revelations. It often operates by way of insight, leapfrogging over more arduous, time-consuming paths on its way to knowledge.

The intensity of such flashes of understanding, allowing things to fall into place abruptly, is uncannily sudden—in this sense, consciousness seems to be able to make risky, yet successful, jumps that are wholly unprecedented. It is as if the brain knows more than we think it does. Insight combines speed and accuracy to make for a radical, almost mysterious, shift in thinking, actually restructuring the cells of the brain in the process.

Mark Jung-Beeman, a cognitive neuroscientist at Northwestern University, has marked out three phases of insight through studying people as they solve word puzzles. In the first problem-solving phase, the mind readies itself by blocking out distractions: the prefrontal cortex and anterior cingulate cortex—or executive control areas—are busily involved, while the sensory areas, like the visual cortex, are suppressed. This is not unlike the way someone might pull down the blind of a window in order to concentrate at a desk. The search stage, which follows, uses additional areas of the brain—in the case of solving word puzzles,

---

**18** Emily Dickinson, "It Was Not Death, For I Stood Up," *The New Pocket Anthology of American Verse*, ed. Oscar Williams (1955, rpt. New York: Pocket Books, Simon & Schuster, 1972), 126.

employing areas related to speech and language—as if the brain were being swept by the executive control area. All this occurs very swiftly, and often people reach an impasse within a few seconds. If nothing comes right away, the best course of action for them is to do something altogether different, such as going for a walk or having a hot shower. This period of relaxation, a movement away from intent concentration upon a problem, appears to allow the brain to continue turning it over at a deeper level of consciousness. If a solution occurs to a person, it arrives as a breakthrough: immediately, the brain seems to recognize the validity of the insight, without having verified it.[19]

And it's nothing short of a burst of fireworks: "three hundred milliseconds before a participant [in the study] offered an answer, the EEG registered a spike of gamma rhythm, which is the highest electrical frequency generated by the brain.... It's as if the insight had gone incandescent."[20] When researchers examined the participants' EEGs, they discovered that the anterior superior temporal gyrus, or aSTG, located in the right hemisphere of the brain, became a sort of switched-on light bulb in the second before the insight occurred. This region is linked to such areas of language comprehension as the interpretation of metaphors, while a related area is involved in the processing of jokes—not surprising, perhaps, given that the subjects were working on word puzzles. But apparently, in the

---

**19** Mark Jung-Beeman in Jonah Lehrer, "The Eureka Hunt: Why do good ideas come to us when they do?" in *The New Yorker* (New York: Condé Nast Publications, July 28, 2008), vol. LXXXIV, no. 22, 42–43. **20** Jonah Lehrer, ibid, 43.

course of any insight, the aSTG allows for unique connections that link distant areas of the brain, so that we can see, sharply and swiftly, not just the trees, but the whole forest. In fact, Jung-Beeman points out that the cells of the right hemisphere are more "broadly tuned ... collecting information from a larger area of cortical space [than those of the left hemisphere]."[21] While the cells of the left hemisphere are more precise, the cells of the right hemisphere put the pieces together, connecting them in order to make discovery possible. No wonder that insight comes to us with the unprecedented force of an epiphany.

The making of connections between distant and disparate things turns out to be the serendipitous way of insight. And it may not be confined to humans—the world and its wild places may operate just as the brain does. If we consider all that is below, around, and above us as the space in which things are constantly becoming linked together in patterns, whether we know it or not, we might be able to understand the world more clearly as an interrelated web, and see ourselves more distinctly as participants in it. And if there is a kind of tawny thinking that is going on all around us, we can appreciate ourselves as inhabitants within a rich and complex biosphere that is fully animated, with strange but plausible lines of communication humming between living things. And why shouldn't this thinking be going on under

**21** Mark Jung-Beeman, ibid, 43.

our very noses, in ways that are utterly indiscernible to us? Or why shouldn't it reveal itself in strange flashes?

Take, for instance, the process of mitosis, in which chromosomes are separated in the cell nucleus to form an identical pair of daughter nuclei. By way of cytokinesis, which follows hard on the heels of this first separation, two new cells, each with its own nucleus, are created. But the parent cell has to make a copy of the chromosomes before cell division takes place, ensuring that the genetic code is kept intact. The very fact of cell division, which occurs as part of the movement of growth, is itself profoundly enigmatic. It is as if the cells of all plants, creatures, and humans are thinking their way into being, and ensuring, by means of a genetic code, or cellular memory, that what springs forth in the future will resemble that of the past. And the actual process, from prophase through to telophase, is remarkably like the leaping nature of insight, as if disorganized ideas were gradually gathering and winnowing and reinventing themselves in bursts of extraordinary clarity. It is a kind of explosive thinking—tawny thinking—happening at the level of life itself.

Poetry takes this tawny thinking into account. And it is often at the edge of language, where syntax begins to slip from order into disorder, that poems make their appearance. The insights of poetry occur at the edges of transformation, where a cell splits, or where words slide into silence. This is part of the reason why poetry reaches out towards other-than-human thinking and other-than-human language: a way of speaking that is impure, tangled, brawny, brambled. This is language turned out of the house. From the unfamiliar hoots of an owl, the shriek of a blue jay, or the discreet mourning of the dove come the curious enigmas of language, a voicing of life that isn't understood, but, nonetheless, weirdly comprehended.

Because of this interest in what lies just beyond knowing, the individual concerns of the poet—any poet—are not necessarily poetry's chief concerns. It is not primarily interested in the self. And its point of view is not singular. It embraces a wider field, with a range of points of view, and a plurality of languages. But even this layered, many-voiced language, full of fecundity, may not be enough. Outside the realm of language is an infinitude that can't be embraced, as in those moments when "a hundred and fifty / psalms pass through the twilight." And so, finally, there is a movement in poetry to relinquish its purpose, to give up the endless work of conveying, of carrying. It directs its energies away from the self, to the place where it verges on the non-self. It points us to the selfless.

Returning to "The Snow Man," we find that the listener is most alive in the very moment of recognizing his own effacement. There is exquisite soundlessness in this moment, for the listener seems to be paying close heed to the fact of his existence being called into question. At the end of these lines there is a quiet in the falling snow that surpasses the written word. For as we come to the limits of language, where poetry desires to pass into silence, we also come to a place where the self begins to pass away—for who can speak of the self when speech itself is vanishing into nothingness?

The thresholding nature of poetry, which allows it to

reveal more than one possibility at the same time, is the reason why it requires plenitude as much as silence. It shows the way to one world, but it keeps a door open to another. It recognizes and can make use of conventional grammar while at the same time employing a telegraphed language, one that may dispense with connectors, like conjunctions, or words and phrases that help make transitions and summarize ideas. While it is language at its most vibrant and dense, it is also, paradoxically, language on its way to silence. In visual terms, it needs the spare whiteness of the page—an untouched emptiness—to contrast language in its fullness with the greater austerity of wordlessness. In aural terms, it holds a pause like the interval of stillness in music before a melody begins again: charged language that comes in bursts followed by stillness. If it were not this way, it would not have such an impact; it would not haunt us with its reverberations.

⊰⊰•⊱⊱

Not long ago, I went back to the Fairmont. At the end of August, after several weeks of cloud and rain, parts of the path were so overgrown as to be impassable. Rosehips hung, lantern-like, from the wild rose bushes. Queen Anne's lace, goldenrod, asters. Poplars rustled in a light wind; it was cool at that dusky hour of the day. The dogs went in wayward directions, but always came back to the track; I followed them up to a bench, honouring a boy whose family had dedicated it to his memory, that overlooked St. George's Bay, and sat there, gazing out over the ocean. Evening's calm.

Over Seabright, a single eagle was gliding in slow circles, hunting. Higher up, on the ridge, the barred owl would be on the lookout for food. In a moment, I knew I'd get up and follow the trail a little higher into the woods, but for now I was mesmerized. Below, above, all around—a hundred and fifty psalms at twilight.

out the cabin window — summer morning

# *Season of Ice*

One winter evening, several years ago, I drove out to a friend's cottage at Cribbon's Beach, north of town. He'd offered to lead a group of us in shamanic journeying; I'd never done such a thing before, but was prepared to try it. We sat in the living room of the cottage, getting acquainted, while a flickering of snow pattered against the window. The parameters of the journey were described to us: we would make a descent into the earth, emerge from it and wait for the arrival of an animal. The animal might or might not appear, but if it revealed itself, we could journey with it.

At the time, I hadn't read much about shamanism. It was only later that I came across the words of Nalungiaq, an Inuit woman. She says that in the "earliest time," people could become animals and animals could become people. As well, they understood one another:

> All spoke the same language.
> That was the time when words were like magic.
> The human mind had mysterious powers.
> A word spoken by chance
> might have strange consequences.
> It would suddenly come alive

> and what people wanted to happen could happen—
> all you had to do was say it.
> Nobody could explain this:
> That's the way it was.[1]

"All spoke the same language"—these words imply a commonality of language between separate spheres. It is exactly such an interpenetration of spheres that is depicted in "Skyworld, Middleworld and the Underworld," a linocut by Ahmoo Ahneesheenahpay, an Ojibway artist from Sioux Lookout, Ontario. The figures of humans and animals in the linocut appear as pale spirits against the intersecting worlds of sky, earth, and sea. The largest of the three human figures has a hole in the middle of his chest, as if to allow things to pass through his skin. We are given a world in which the realm of the human is integrated with that of the animal, just as the mythical is integrated with the real.

The shamanic journey, too, I came to see, reveals a deep desire to move towards wholeness and integration. What would be learned, and risked, on such a journey? We went downstairs and sat in a circular room or kiva, based on an ancient Pueblo Indian design. My friend lit a smudge and brushed the smoke before each of us, then sat down and began drumming. All of us lay still on the floor of the kiva. My eyes were closed; my ears were filled with the regular

---

1 Nalungiaq, trans. Knud Rasmussen, in Jerome Rothenberg and Diane Rothenberg, *Symposium of the Whole: A Range of Discourses toward an Ethnopoetics*, cited by David Abram, *The Spell of the Sensuous: Perception and Language in a More-Than-Human World* (1996, rpt. New York: Vintage Books, 1997), 87.

sound of the drum. I was also aware of the breathing of the others. The man beside me promptly fell asleep and I wanted to laugh, but after quite a long time, distracted as I was, I found a way into the earth, penetrating its thick gloom, and it seemed I was descending by way of a passage. When I reached level ground at the bottom, the darkness thickened, but now I saw hundreds of small flames. A sound like the rustling of leaves. Ghost voices.

I was between the living and the dead in an underworld. It took time to become calm, so I could proceed. At last I came out of that place, surfacing into a world of brilliance: it seemed to be Antigonish Harbour, ice-white, flanked by snow-covered hills. I went forward to an island of slim birches and spruce, and saw a bird apparently cut from the whiteness of the clouds. This shape flew before me. I followed, realizing that it was a snowy owl.

The movement into darkness and then up and into the dazzle of light is a visionary passage that is intense, strange, and even prophetic. The poet Laurie Sheck points out: "The underworld [is] a place of seeing, but the seeing is turned inward.... This is why Persephone must come back for a part of each year to the surface of the earth—to feel the tension between the world outside her body and the world within."[2] Persephone is a split figure, one who exists between death and life. Like her, poets find themselves in a

---

2 Laurie Sheck in *The Poet's Notebook: Excerpts from the Notebooks of Contemporary American Poets*, eds. Stephen Kuusisto et al. (New York: W.W. Norton & Co., 1995), 263.

chiaroscuro of light and darkness, employing forked words they bring back from the shadows.

I spent hours walking the ice of Antigonish Harbour during the winter I first learned about shamanic journeys. On one occasion I walked east from the Landing towards Williams' Point, past the ice-fishing huts. It was as though I was walking on clouds. It usually took me less than a half an hour to reach one of the islands off Williams' Point. Spruce and white pines grew there, and I always hoped to see a bald eagle in the branches of the dead elm near the point. The dogs were jubilant as they galloped over the island, and then ran back to me, lopsidedly, ears flapping. One Labrador was black and glossy, the other golden-brown.

I made my way around the island, and turned back, walking in the direction of a ridge crowned by a smoothly shaped hill. Sugarloaf, the remnant of an old volcano, presided over the harbour like a broad-shouldered giant; below it were the snow-dusted slopes of Bekker's farm. What is it that sets winter apart? It might have had something to do with the season's sere clarity, shorn of clutter. My writing too, during those months, cut to the bone; winter allowed for a different kind of seeing. A mature eagle lifted up and flew over Kennedy's farm and I watched it glide in slow, almost languid circles, as it searched for food. The world was achingly bright. I could have stayed outside all day, but the dogs, back on the scent, were impatient to go home, and I followed them, thinking how I was drawn onto the wide-open, frozen harbour because of the abundance of the light that reflected off the ice.

footprints in snow
(+ pawprints)
Antigonish Harbour

Once, before sunrise, I drove out to the Antigonish Landing and walked from the car out onto the ice. The morning was windless and clear, and snow lay in a thin covering over the harbour. No one was around. No sound could be heard. As the first light spilled into the world, I lay down, filled up with the lavishness of dawn. The snow was spangled with rubies, emeralds, sapphires. Glints of amber and topaz. It seemed as if I could see farther. Overwhelmed by beauty, I was also aware of loss, since what I saw would always surpass me. Any attempt to get nearer to it would make it recede further.

⊰•⊱

But poetry is the attempt to salvage what has slipped away. The poet finds herself in a liminal state, and tries to bring a shadowy, elusive strangeness into the ordinary world. Surely this otherness is the very pith of life—or what Lorca calls *duende*. It is, he says, "the mystery ... which furnishes us with whatever is sustaining in art.... The *duende*, then, is a power and not a construct, is a struggle and not a concept."[3]

*Duende* cannot be explained as something static, but as something dynamic. It is realized in the midst of a struggle, but this struggle might also be thought of as a process. So it is fluid, in movement, or in process—it is animated. Whoever possesses *duende* has to be open to risking oblivion, while at the same time resisting it. Indeed, *duende* has

**3** Federico Garcia Lorca, *In Search of Duende*, ed. and trans. Christopher Maurer (New York: New Directions, 1998) 48–49.

much to do with desire, which is inherent in such a struggle. Desire is dynamic, moving between absence and presence. Since it is consistently frustrated from resting, the structure of a never-ending struggle is sustained. Such a structure depends on the idea that two poles, or two people—Orpheus and Eurydice, for example—remain distinct and identifiable. Once they merge, dissolve, or join, desire dissipates. Without a struggle, or the risk of destruction, there can be no *duende*.

Poetry shapes itself around desire, the pith of life, and because it is shaped in this way the wildness inherent in it cannot be duplicated. In the following computer-generated poem, it is the lack of *duende* that becomes most apparent, despite the clumsy gesturing towards desire:

> the delicate kiss fell quickly
> the fire fondled a heartbroken mouth
> the flame shouted tenderly you loved us
> a fragile passion kissed us …

And so on. The poem, which has no title, though it is numbered, was created by a digital poetry generator that "randomly originates lyrical pieces of semi-erotic content written in blank verse series of ten lines."[4]

But desire is a powerful force. It can't be reduced in this way. And it shouldn't be thought of as something that is

---

**4** N. Millan, "Computer Generated Poetry and the Arts," M. Sc. Dissertation in Computer Science (Birmingham, UK: The University of Birmingham, September 2001).

confined to the lover and the beloved. It could manifest itself as an address, redolent with longing, to the land, or the creatures of the land, as in this fragment of a poem by Tim Lilburn:

> Listen, listen.
> Three years ago, when the gold animal appeared to me,
> a small combed sun, thin road, and took my smell,
> it walked out of the robes of its custom
> and it bent and took my smell.
> It came very quickly out of the trees from
> the palmed night place, the
> west, the labour-field, and lay down in the fire of my smell ...[5]

The gold animal and the small combed sun of this poem haunt me with their foreign, luminous beauty. The weirdness of the wild is always a challenge to the human. "Lonely land," says the poet Alison Pick, "and if you go there you will become more lonely."[6] The wild exceeds us. It is *more than*. It astonishes; it terrifies. To go towards nature is to move, or try to move, to the very limits of the human.

This can be perilous: to press forward is to risk one's sanity. Thresholds may be reached by means of intoxication, dream or insomnia, or states of ecstasy, depression, madness. But if there is to be inspiration, access is needed to what lies beyond the known. This reaching from the known to the dimly perceived is what gives literature its impetus.

---

**5** Tim Lilburn, "Now, Lifted, Now," in *Kill-site* (Toronto, ON: McClelland & Stewart, 2003), 75. **6** Alison Pick, from an unpublished line in a poem originally titled "Horseshoe Cliff."

Alain Toumayan says that "like death, inspiration is ultimately a relation with otherness."[7]

⊰·•·⊱

If we could make a figure that represented desire, it would be metaphor. It reaches out, yearning for what lies beyond, but like an unrequited lover, it never gets what it wants. Metaphor is always necessarily open. I can take the example of a sunflower, and describe it, adequately enough, as a flower native to the Americas, but metaphor reinvents it as a clock; when I think about it as a clock, I'm jolted, momentarily, out of my usual thinking.

Instead of showing what-is, metaphor offers what-could-be, bringing these things together and letting them glimmer and glint. For a mere instant, I slide back and forth between what I'm certain I know and what I realize I don't know. Without even thinking about it, I return to what I know — the sunflower, or *Helianthus annuus*, is a heavy-headed flower on a tall stalk, whose seeds can be processed for oil. How can the description, and, indeed, representation, of the thing called "sunflower" be false? But the possibility that it might not be true remains, disrupting the familiar. And allowing for possibilities is the very work of metaphor.

Trickster-like, metaphor's *modus operandi* is to swing alongside something else, indulging in an impossibly agile,

---

**7** Alain P. Toumayan, *Encountering the Other: The Artwork and the Problem of Difference in Blanchot and Levinas* (Pittsburgh, PA: Duquesne University Press, 2004), 99.

acrobatic move, and slipping off before we have time to absorb it. In so doing, metaphor reveals to us that anything at all, from sunflowers to clocks, can be questioned. It points out how the truth of things is in no way fixed, and that language too, representing these things, is both flexible and fallible. Metaphor fails, ultimately, in a spectacular way, because it cannot fasten upon, take hold of, or possess. But this so-called failure is also its success. If metaphor shows us how little we know about sunflowers, exploring and examining the way we represent them, it also makes clear that otherness is a mystery of such infinitude that we cannot describe it.

The example of the sunflower-as-clock is a simplistic investigation of metaphor, which is vastly more complex. Still, it's this two-sided figure of metaphor on which attention has been concentrated. Metaphor has been regarded, traditionally, as a method of comparison that departs from the literal, or a figure that makes a flourish as it deviates from conventional language. Aristotle describes metaphor as transference, or giving something a name that belongs to something else.[8] This is clear enough: a clock is not the name given to a sunflower. And the ability on the part of the poet to have a command of metaphor, is deemed, by Aristotle, as "the greatest thing by far." But he also says that metaphor is a deviation from usual language, and that clarity consists in replacing strange words or metaphors with

---

**8** Aristotle, from *Poetics*, in *The Complete Works of Aristotle: The Revised Oxford Translation* (Bollingen series; 71:2), ed. Jonathan Barnes (1984, rpt. Princeton, NJ: Princeton University Press, 1995), 2332.

"ordinary words ... to see the truth of what we are saying."[9] The suggestion is that metaphor evades truth.

But truth may be as elusive as metaphor. Nietzsche questions whether such a thing as pure truth can exist. He notes that "the 'thing-in-itself' (which would be, precisely, pure truth ...) is impossible for even the creator of language to grasp...."[10] Even if pure truth exists, Nietzsche inquires, where is that pure vessel—the inhuman language—in which it resides? He points out that "we believe that when we speak of trees, colours, snow, and flowers, we have knowledge of the things themselves, and yet we possess only metaphors of things which in no way correspond to the original entities."[11] For Nietzsche, there is no absolute truth on which to rely; nevertheless, language is charged with the task of presenting this truth. Language is inherently metaphorical, he says, because it is basic to our thinking: "that drive to form metaphors, that fundamental human drive which cannot be left out of consideration for even a second without also leaving out human beings themselves, is in truth not defeated."[12]

Both Aristotle and Nietzsche are in agreement about the fact that overused, or dead, metaphors lack innovation. As Nietzsche points out, a worn-out metaphor takes on rigidity and "finally acquires the same significance for all human

---

**9** Ibid, 2334. **10** Friedrich Nietzsche, "On Truth and Lying in a Non-Moral Sense," in *The Birth of Tragedy and Other Writings* (*Cambridge Texts in the History of Philosophy*), eds. Raymond Geuss and Ronald Speirs, trans. Ronald Speirs (Cambridge, UK: Cambridge University Press, 1999), 144.
**11** Ibid, 144. **12** Ibid, 150–151.

beings, as if it were the only necessary image."[13] Aristotle says that "ordinary words convey only what we know already; it is from metaphor that we can best get hold of something fresh."[14]

But in Thomas Hobbes's *Leviathan*, all metaphors are misleading, whether fresh or old: "they are *ignes fatui;* and reasoning upon them is wandering amongst innumerable absurdities; and their end, contention and sedition, or contempt."[15] John Locke, in his *Essay Concerning Human Understanding*, extends this thinking, excoriating figurative language: not only is it contemptible, it is antagonistic to the truth. So metaphor is given the full scorched-earth treatment.

Fortunately, poets have paid no attention. Yet the view of metaphor that prevailed until well into the twentieth century, largely based on Aristotle's *Poetics*, takes for granted that the things being compared in metaphor have prior existence; that metaphor may be translated; and that metaphor's real purpose is to enhance language.[16] Breaking with this, I.A. Richards says that metaphor operates by bringing together the "vehicle," or sunflower, with the "tenor," or clock. (I can never seem to remember which is which—is the vehicle a taxi for the tenor?) What is clear is that Richards describes metaphor by using metaphor. He does point out, helpfully, that metaphor is a figuring of language that

---

**13** Ibid, 149. **14** Aristotle, from *Rhetoric*, in George Lakoff and Mark Johnson, *Metaphors We Live By* (Chicago, IL: University of Chicago Press, 1980), 190. **15** Thomas Hobbes, *Leviathan*, in George Lakoff and Mark Johnson, 190. **16** M.H. Abrams, *A Glossary of Literary Terms*, 7th Ed. (1985, rpt. Orlando, FL: Harcourt Brace College Publishers, 1999), 155.

can't be translated literally. It's an interaction that sparks meaning as a consequence: it isn't just poetic decoration, or rhetorical departure.[17]

So this was a turn in thinking, but it took Max Black, a mathematician and musician, as well as a philosopher, to expand on these ideas. Black says that the process of making a metaphor, with a cluster of complex associations brought together with another such cluster, is a "distinctive *intellectual* operation." Instead of assuming that similarity exists prior to the metaphor, Black says "it would be more illuminating in some of these cases to say that the metaphor *creates* the similarity."[18] This may have opened the way for the view that divisions between literal and metaphorical language are artificial, and that ordinary language is shot through with metaphor. The very fabric of our thinking allows us to consider things metaphorically.

—•—

When the small group of us learned about shamanic journeys several years ago, we were instructed to ask an animal a question, should the animal appear to us. The question I asked the snowy owl, a question that is no longer exact in my mind, had to do with suffering. It was something like this: "What should we do about suffering?" There was no bell-ringing answer. With my eyes shut, nothing came to me. There was only whiteness, a few bare birches and

---

**17** Ibid, 155. **18** Max Black, "Metaphor," *Proceedings of the Aristotelian Society* (London: The Aristotelian Society, 1955), 273–294.

spruce trees on snow-covered islands. I could see plainly across the icy vista of the harbour, and it seemed that the question reverberated in the cold air.

What should we do?

It was only afterwards that I understood that the frost-white landscape, with its own subtle language, was itself an answer. We left the kiva that night, thanked our host, and made our way home along the harbour road with a light snow falling. A week, or perhaps two weeks, passed, and then came the kind of news that rips apart tightly connected communities—a boy had committed suicide. He had been in grade twelve at the local high school. I hadn't known him, though I was acquainted with his mother. Like so many others, I went to the funeral to support the family, and found the church packed to overflowing. There were fine, strong voices singing. The boy's hockey teammates shambled forward in the way of teenagers who were used to laughing and fooling around, but who were now shocked into silence. Their coach was with them, shadows under his eyes. And then the coffin, with its young pallbearers. The boys' parents, stricken.

I went to the Landing for an hour or so each day for several weeks after that, walking on the ice with the dogs, but I found I couldn't get the boy's suicide out of my mind. Something had to be written, I knew, but I didn't know how to write it. Words could only provide a makeshift hut on the ice, a crude shelter. At such times, it seems to be empathy that fires imagination, not voyeurism. It is an effort to offer witness. But imagination can be relentless. I wrestled with what I wrote, because I didn't particularly want to do it.

The experience was brutal—I learned how a person dies by hanging; I learned how long it takes, depending on how far and how fast a person falls. If the fall is short, then the dying is more agonizing and drawn-out. If the fall is long, then the time it takes to die is brief. I found myself thinking about the boy, imagining him in the garage with a coil of rope, or an orange extension cord, trying not to wake his parents as he took off his boots and got up on a chair, an old table saw, or a broken dryer.

As I began to write, the figure of an old woman came to me: she was weird, in the sense of the old Anglo-Saxon word, *wyrd*, which has to do with fate (as the word is used, for instance, in the epic poem *Beowulf*), rather than eccentricity. She seemed at once human and animal. I didn't know why she was there, only that she had arrived in the poem and wasn't going to leave it. Because of her, I wrote my way through the boy's preparations, through his dying, through his death. I wrote my way through the holes in his socks, the laces of his boots. I wrote through his young body to the place where there was nothing left. And at that point the old woman picked up his spirit, light as a feather, and took it away with her. She was, I thought, a healer.

Much later, I realized that the ordeal of writing this poem was the very struggle about which Lorca writes. I was brushing against the spirits of the dead as I wrote, trying to find a way to witness the unspeakable. The struggle seemed monumental.

But the alternative—not to write—didn't seem to be an option.

⊰⊰•⊱⊱

Snow on
spruce + tombstones

Metaphor is not simply a figure; metaphor is the *way* of a poem, revealing a relationship in which something calls to another. When I wrote the poem about the boy and the old woman, I had no idea that each of them called forth the other. I only knew that I could write the poem after the old woman appeared. Imagination summoned the one who had the power to heal, just as imagination had given me the suffering of the unknown boy, the one who had the power to destroy himself.

"The poem intends another, needs this other, needs an opposite," says Paul Celan. "It goes toward it, bespeaks it."[19] Not only can the poem call to those outside the poem—those who attend, listening—it can also speak to the other, or multiple others, within the poem itself. Metaphor depends on relationship; it is no wonder that it calls out to otherness. By sustaining the integrity of distinct voices, or distinct things, it reveals how they are connected, "the way this world can be known by pushing / against it. And feeling something pushing back."[20]

Something pushes; something pulls. This is the nature of metaphor. There is no subordination in its formulation; it proceeds by what is called, in grammatical terms, parataxis. A paratactical sentence doesn't show how things are related causally, as in: "It will soon snow because the air has grown colder." It merely juxtaposes one thing with another: "Snow; small baskets of cold." It doesn't set up an

---

**19** Paul Celan, in Gerald L. Bruns, *Maurice Blanchot: The Refusal of Philosophy* (Baltimore, MD: The Johns Hopkins University Press, 1997), 96. **20** Jack Gilbert, "The White Heart of God," *The Great Fires* (New York: Alfred A. Knopf, 2001), 46.

asymmetrical relationship; it doesn't set up a hierarchical relationship. Metaphor works in a similar way. Since it dispenses with the kind of markers that show one thing to be greater than, or less than, another, metaphor does not judge. It allows for things to be equal.

So the disparate parts of metaphor don't dissolve into one, nor does the conjunction of parts result in something new, like offspring from a marriage. Yet the two aspects of metaphor, consistently separate, are part of something larger. Maurice Merleau-Ponty could be speaking of metaphor when he speaks of dialectical thought, which is:

> capable of differentiating and of integrating into one sole universe the double or even multiple meanings, as Heraclitus has already showed us [through] opposite directions coinciding in the circular movement.... [It] is capable of effecting this integration because the circular movement is neither the simple sum of the opposed movements nor a third movement added to them, but their common meaning, the two component movements visible as one sole movement....[21]

He makes clear that neither of the opposed movements creates a third; instead, they participate as two parts of what he calls "one sole movement." This is what creates the dynamic of the dialectical. It's the push-pull shape of poetry: two movements within one.

---

**21** Maurice Merleau-Ponty, *The Visible and the Invisible,* trans. Alphonso Lingis (Evanston, IL: Northwestern University Press, 1968), 191–192.

The question of what we should do about suffering still sounds in my mind. I'm not sure that poetry can do very much of anything to alleviate it. The only thing it can do is point to pain, or point beyond pain, but it can't stop it. It does, however, allow for the possibility of change.

Paul Ricoeur says, "metaphor shatters not only previous structures of our language, but also shatters the previous structures of what we call reality."[22] It shatters reality: this is its gift to us. So, inevitably, the making that is my task as a writer is also an unmaking. That winter, it led me back to the ice-covered harbour, where, on the island, a sprinkling of snow fell from a tree branch and drifted away. Whatever I had written was as nothing in the face of a boy committing suicide. It simply revealed a wish to understand. It revealed care. "What is changed by poetic dwelling," Ricoeur goes on to say, "is our way of dwelling in the world. Each poem projects a new way of dwelling.... It opens up a new way of being for us."[23] It is as if through struggling through the darkest places of imagination, we are astonished by a reprieve, when it comes.

We can't change suffering, but we can go through it, making a descent not unlike that made by Virgil and Dante in the *Inferno.* When these poets emerge from having been deep in the land of the dead, they see the night sky with a clarity they did not possess before. They stand poised between

**22** Paul Ricoeur, "Word, Polysemy, Metaphor: Creativity in Language," trans. David Pellauer, reprinted from *Philosophy Today* 17, 2–4 (Summer 1973), 97–128. This article was reprinted in *A Ricoeur Reader: Reflection and Imagination,* ed. Mario J. Valdés (Toronto, ON: University of Toronto Press, 1991), 65–85. **23** Ibid, 85.

worlds, hardly daring to breathe, as if they were waking—still trembling—from a nightmare. They stand gazing at the stars. Just as Virgil and Dante's journey through hell is outside time, so too is this instant, shivering with ecstasy.

I often return to something I read a few years ago in *The Poet's Notebook*. The poet Cynthia MacDonald talks about the reading of a translation of Dante's *Inferno* at the 92nd Street Y in New York City, describing the event. At one point, she mentions Rebecca Sinkler's review of the event in *The New York Times Book Review:*

> Mr. Hass ... paused ... increasing the tension and drama in the last moments of the poem, then delivered the last lines of the last stanza: Dante and Virgil emerging from hell, glimpsing 'the night sky with the beautiful things it carries / And we came out and looked up at the stars.'[24]

Cynthia MacDonald continues, speaking of the audience, "And we came out and looked up at a starless New York sky, we who had journeyed for four hours in the company of poets and the beautiful things they carry."[25]

The wordlessness of the poem's ending is palpably enlarged by astonishment. It is a silence, yes, but one that is filled with wonder and possibility. And I like to think that this is not just Virgil and Dante's experience: this is also what poetry gives its audience. It sends us back to the

---

**24** Rebecca Sinkler in *The Poet's Notebook: Excerpts from the Notebooks of Contemporary American Poets*, eds. Stephen Kuusisto et al. (New York: W.W. Norton & Co., 1995), 171. **25** Cynthia MacDonald, ibid, 171.

world, but it sends us back as different people. We are—or we should be—shaken, stunned, surprised by the night sky, by the beautiful things it carries.

## A WOMAN, AN OWL, A BOY

A woman. Weir of bone holding a fish-glimmering
heart, feather-tufted ear, night heel, marked
with a star.

Lying on the ice. A woman.

Comes gliding, mute, an owl. Shorn eyes
tuned to the world, ice dazzled.

Clutched water. Cold. Layers of pale
jade. Below, the living, the dying. In their throats,
dry leaves are rasping. Ear
to her own body, a woman folds back
one skin, another.

Hears a boy, hands tightening a necklace of rope. Hears
him kick away the chair.

Hears the world stopped at the rope.

Her eyes fill with tears.

The owl finds her,
flies into her mouth as she asks a question.

The rope
with a mother at one end,
child at the other.

Gone into the unstarred dark
of her mouth, the owl glides
until the woman sees

with topaz eyes. Until she moves noiselessly,
lifts into air.

Yanked. Held.

She's held by air. Hears silence, its shape

and smell.
Flies to the top of the white pine. An owl listening
at the nape of light.

Hears the boy, each burned
minute, skin against rope, rope
against skin, neck unsnapped. Kicking, he
kicks back into childhood. Claws, with both hands,
back through
brother, sister, cousin—

long:::the knot:::the knotted breath:::furious lack:::

the seconds exploding for lack no mother no father no
bell of air in the lungs no feet no earth no walking
no mother no father no bell of

She hears the last, the gone.

Stillness, that velvet, around a child's body.

Hanging, feet in socks, hole in the right heel.

Stillness. Boots below, side by side.

A woman finds herself lying on ice, as if fallen.
Lying on a bed of radiance, wingless,
in the bone weir of body.

Hears daylight's
howling.

Opens her eyes, gets up,
holding the body of a boy, an owl feather
against her ribs.

Takes it with her.

# *Looking at Paintings*

In the summer of 1998, while visiting my parents' home in Ontario, I discovered a painting. It was not the first time I'd seen it, but it was the first time I'd paid it any attention: the *Isenheim Altarpiece* was painted by sixteenth-century German artist Matthias Grünewald, about whom little is known. Another German artist and historian, Joachim von Sandrart, who published the first biographical study of Grünewald more than a century later, saddled him with the wrong name—Grünewald's real name may have been Mathis Gothardt Nithardt.[1] To add insult to injury, Grünewald was overshadowed by his more famous countryman, Albrecht Dürer, with whom he has sometimes been confused.

In fact, when I first began looking for a reproduction of the *Isenheim Altarpiece*, I thought Dürer had painted it. But Grünewald was capable of creating wholly original work, culminating in the *Isenheim Altarpiece*, now on display in the Musée d'Unterlinden in Colmar, which lies in Alsace, France, near the German border. Thought to have been

---

1 E.H. Gombrich, *The Story of Art* (1950, rpt., London: Phaidon Press, 1972), 268.

painted between 1512 and 1516, the altarpiece was originally commissioned for the chapel of a hospital and monastery belonging to the Antonite Order in Isenheim, a village near Colmar. The hospital specialized in cures for those afflicted with ergotism, or St. Anthony's Fire, a painful disease contracted by those who ate rye bread tainted with a poisonous fungus.[2]

The book in which I recalled seeing the painting was still on my parents' bookshelf in exactly the place I remembered. Beautifully reproduced, the altarpiece was printed over several pages which could be folded into panels. These opened to reveal each of the paintings—a sort of pop-up version of the entire altarpiece. I could see precisely how it had been constructed to be read, by those looking at it, like a very large picture book.

I had gone looking for the *Isenheim Altarpiece* because I had read something arresting in Eric Hobsbawm's *The Age of Extremes: The Short Twentieth Century, 1914–1991*. The book begins with "The Century: A Bird's Eye View," in which Isaiah Berlin is quoted as saying "I remember it only as the most terrible century in Western history."[3] Hobsbawm himself observed that the twentieth century could be viewed in three parts, like a triptych.[4] I could see the scenes as he described them, with the cataclysmic era of warfare followed by a period of apparent calm, and this, in turn, giving way to the disquieting *fin de siècle*.

---

**2** Stanley Meisler, "A Masterpiece Born of St. Anthony's Fire," (Washington, DC: *Smithsonian Magazine*, September 1999). **3** Isaiah Berlin in Eric Hobsbawm *The Age of Extremes: The Short Twentieth Century, 1914–1991* (1994, rpt. London: Abacus, 1995), 1. **4** Hobsbawm, ibid, 6.

The notion of a century viewed as a triptych intrigued me. It was 1998, and the end of the twentieth century was imminent. Hobsbawm's idea allowed me to think about the historical implications of the century in an immediate, visual way, one that was succinct and whole, yet separated into sections. The *Isenheim Altarpiece* seemed to exemplify this idea. It appeared to me as a series of depictions, one folded upon the other, showing the events of the twentieth century.

At the same time as I was reading Eric Hobsbawm's book, I was walking early every morning, following the same route, down a street towards Burlington Bay and the view of the steel factories in Hamilton. It was a view I'd known since childhood; a cluster of steel factories owned by rival companies, Stelco and Dofasco (both recently swallowed up by larger ones), crouching dragon-like, at the edge of the water. I continued along Lakeshore Drive, past the large houses, some newly constructed, and some that had been built decades before, to the Burlington Golf & Country Club. Lakeshore Drive bisected the property, with a parking lot and pro shop on one side and the imposing club building on the other. The velvety grass spread across a slope down to the lake, where, in the distance, the stacks and furnaces of the steel factories stood in stark contrast. It seemed to me that this epitomized what we had made of the twentieth century—a factory, a golf course. It was the beginning of a poem.

The poem, which I knew wouldn't be a short one, would

take into consideration the *Isenheim Altarpiece* and the idea of the twentieth century as a triptych. But the golf course would provide a sort of stage for the events of the poem. It gave me a fixed point, a landscape, from which I could veer away and to which I could return, while simultaneously developing jottings and thoughts about the century. I needed a fixed point, since my long poems often threatened to fly off into the ether. I was hard pressed to keep the scatterings together.

This may be because poems of more than a few pages seem to have a built-in tendency to thrust *away* from the central idea or ideas. After auditing a winter course on the long narrative poem given by Demetres Tryphonopoulos at the University of New Brunswick a few years before, I'd begun thinking of this thrusting-away as centrifugal force, which directs something outward like a tetherball (held in check by a rope) swinging around a pole. The outward thrust needs to be countered by an inward thrust, or the centripetal force of the poem. The form of the long poem is partly shaped by these inherent tensions. In the case of "Altarpiece," I found that the structure of the poem depended on this inward pull and outward push. I was pulled inward by my thoughts about Grünewald's altarpiece, which seemed inextricably connected to my thoughts about the twentieth century, and I was pushed outward into the manicured landscape of the golf course. I moved back and forth between these things, gradually realizing what it was I wanted to say.

Poetry is thinking that takes a particular, compressed

shape, and I was beginning to grope towards that shape with a triad of ideas. I would take up one idea, consider it, remember another idea, consider it: the process was like picking up stones on a beach. Once I'd gathered things together I began to see the whole. But there was a great deal I couldn't see at the time. Much later, long after the poem was written, I realized that I was making blocks of text on each page, and that these blocks were like short films, containing vivid, flashing pictures of events, like old-fashioned newsreels. I was creating my own version of an altarpiece, without knowing that was what I was doing. I don't think I was trying to make something that resembled the *Isenheim Altarpiece*. What Grünewald had done was far beyond me; still, it seemed that I was charged to respond to this particular work of art. What stopped the flotsam and jetsam of the poem from being flung away in a centrifugal thrust as I pursued the writing were the images from this altarpiece, which seemed to solidify it.

⁂

What I was doing, in my groping toward a poem, was employing *ekphrasis*, a Greek word, in which "*ek*" means "out," and "*phrasis*" means "to speak." But this doesn't really illuminate *ekphrasis;* it is only when we discover that it was a rhetorical tool used by the Greeks to describe art or artifacts—like the long, eloquent description of Achilles' shield in Homer's *Iliad* (XVIII: 594–739)—that it becomes clearer. James Heffernan elaborates on the meaning of *ekphrasis*, explaining that it is the "verbal representation of graphic representation."[5] Both literature and art involve representations of reality, translating it, and giving it back to us in sharpened, heightened, or compressed form.

Since literature *speaks* of art, a relation is established. One speaks of the other. The risk is that literature might be seen as having a merely interpretative role, in the sense of a publicist trumpeting the merits of art. Heffernan is quick to disagree with the idea that a poem merely "aspires to the atemporal 'eternity' of the stopped-action painting...." Instead, he says, "ekphrastic literature typically delivers *from* the pregnant moment of graphic art ... and thus makes explicit the story that graphic art tells only by implication."[6] The work of literature is able to speak, we are told, while the work of art implies. Literature apparently dominates by virtue of its access to language. Is this the way we should regard either the poem or the work of art? Rather than emphasizing the dynamic play that is at work between poetry and art, we are reduced to choosing sides.

It may be useful to look at the relationship between word and image in another way. What is it about the work of art that brings poets close, compelling them to speak of it, accommodate it, and allow for its potent, and possibly disruptive, potential? Perhaps it has to do with the power of the work of art, which is so similar to that of poetry, in the way it holds time in abeyance, interrupting it. As Gerald

---

**5** James Heffernan, "Ekphrasis and Representation," *New Literary History*, Vol. 22, No. 2, Spring (Baltimore, MD: The Johns Hopkins University Press, 1991), 299. **6** Ibid, 301.

Bruns says: "an image … takes hold of us, grips us. Whoever is confronted by an image is no longer a being-in-the-world."[7] This idea, that we are no longer in the world when we encounter the image, points to the way art transports us out of the ordinary. We can't resist the experience, but at the same time we are dispossessed. Bruns goes on to say this: "Likewise the thing of which it is an image is no longer an object in the world but a thing doubled, shadowed, followed by a semblance of its former self."[8]

When I returned to the *Isenheim Altarpiece* years after I'd written a long poem about it, the notion of the doubling and shadowing inherent in the images became clear to me. Bruns speaks of an image hovering outside the world; and in the same breath he mentions the uncanny ability of the image to replicate itself. In Grünewald's altarpiece, the dying Christ is a version of a known image, shown in a realistic, harrowing way. When the first panels of the altarpiece are opened, the scene of the Crucifixion is replaced by the Nativity, with the infant Christ in the arms of his mother, another well-known image. This miniature Christ is doubled in the adjacent side panel by the spectacularly risen Christ, and shadowed below by the images of the predella, which shows the gruesome body of another Christ being lamented by mourners.

Not only do the images of the altarpiece shadow one another, they appear to us as if from a time beyond time,

---

**7** Gerald L. Bruns, *Maurice Blanchot: The Refusal of Philosophy* (Baltimore, MD: The Johns Hopkins University Press, 1997), 18. **8** Ibid, 18.

a place beyond place. At the same time, each panel of the polyptych reveals an atmosphere of anxiety not unlike the unsettled mood of our own age. I began looking at each of the paintings more closely. In the Crucifixion panel, I was struck by the sheer ugliness of Christ, his skin covered with sores and tinted slightly green. His arms are thin and taut, stretched by the weight of his body, his head lolls to his chest, and his fingers, horribly splayed, resemble broken twigs. The sores speckling his skin show that, in Grünewald's version of events, Christ is suffering from St. Anthony's Fire.

Near the cross, the Virgin Mary swoons into the arms of John the Apostle. Her face is almost as white as her cowl and wimple; she could be lifeless except for the determined gesture of her hands, joined in supplication. Below her is Mary Magdalene, with her hands also raised, fingers like wheeling blades. On the other side of the cross, John the Baptist, back from the dead, points like a didactic professor to the lesson of Christ's suffering. The figures of the Crucifixion panel are dramatic, but even more compelling are the stark shapes they make against a dark background. The anguish of the painting has as much to do with the shape of the Virgin Mary falling back against John the Apostle, with the shape of Christ's fingers, matched by Mary Magdalene's fingers below, and with the shape of John the Baptist's pointing arm. It has to do with the bold and savage colours: red, for both saints, and a paler red for Mary Magdalene, stark white for the Virgin Mary, and velvet blackness behind everything. The flat, dark background is vaguely disturbing, since the figures could be in the middle of a night sky—they are *nowhere*. They aren't of the world. Yet they possess a clarity that makes them seem dazzlingly real, even though they are merely pictures on wood. And they possess this clarity because the emotion they convey is powerfully evident. No one can dispute the devastating grief embodied by the figure of the Virgin Mary.

They may be like us in the depth of their feelings, but they are also wholly, radically unlike us. I realize now that I was attempting to place them in the here and now of a poem so they could offer a contrast to our place, our time. The collision of our ordinary, banal world with these otherworldly figures, undergoing their austere trials, gave me a way to write the poem: they appeared as visionary figures. I let myself be led by them. Still, almost as soon as I beheld them, since I *did* behold them, within the common landscape of the world, they disappeared.

Why does the image seem to disappear before our eyes? Paintings reveal the impasse they try to surmount: some incompletion, or gap, lies within the very thing that any painting attempts to demonstrate. The image can't begin to fulfill its promise—that of revealing the truth of the thing itself. It evades us. The figures in the *Isenheim Altarpiece*—definite, clearly shaped, and rich with colour—spring from nothingness, appearing vividly, only to fade away. The painting appears as a fully realized presence, but concealed within it is a haunting absence.

So does a painting really speak to us? Perhaps it is altogether indifferent to our world. Maurice Blanchot says "the image speaks to us, and seems to speak intimately to us of ourselves."[9] But he goes on to say that the apparent, personal intimacy between image and viewer is destroyed, though the image seems to continue affirming what it represents. How many of us have spent periods of time in galleries enjoying particular works of art, while at the same time sensing such works have projected themselves past us, that they have nothing to do with us? This is unsettling, since it shows us "the menacing proximity of a vague and empty outside, the ... basis upon which it continues to affirm things in their disappearance."[10] The image seems to speak beyond us, towards the vanishing to which we, too, are directed.

Take the Resurrection panel of the altarpiece—Christ bursts out of his tomb and scatters soldiers across the ground as if they were toys. His halo doesn't just circle his head, but his entire body. The garish golds and reds of his garments are cartoon-bright, in contrast to the sombre colours of the soldiers' fallen bodies. Unlike the Crucifixion panel, this Christ isn't meekly submitting to anything. The sheer force of his ascent is explosive. He's not meant to resemble the human, but the divine: no wonder he seems like a figure from the psychedelic art of the 1960s. He brings us to the uncanny. But the uncanny lies on the far side of the ordinary, so a rupture opens up.

The very act of looking at the painting, and making the attempt to cross the gap that always separates us, permits

---

**9** Maurice Blanchot, *The Space of Literature*, trans. Ann Smock (Lincoln, NB: University of Nebraska Press, 1990), 254. **10** Ibid, 254.

us to bring it into the world. Even though it slips outside our place and time, it holds us, momentarily, and we hold it. Like those who suffered from the affliction of St. Anthony's Fire, who must have viewed the altarpiece in the hospital chapel of the Antonite monastery in Isenheim, we absorb the images, like the painting of Christ covered with sores, *into* ourselves, even if we think we have nothing to do with the Christ covered with sores. We do the same thing with the vision of the resurrected Christ, the one who casts off sickness and death to emerge out of the grave like Superman. This figure glows in our minds, in a coming-together that occurs between ourselves and the image, though, at the same time, we remain distant from it.

What is it, then, that we learn about vision, or seeing, by looking at paintings? Do we simply find that every time we gaze at a painting we are drawn in, only to be thrust out and kept at a distance? No, we learn that we can see into a painting, envisioning along *with* the painter, in the sense of accompanying him or her in realizing new worlds. We see and partake of the world just as we see and partake of the painting, letting our eyes inhabit its space. At the same time, we see the painting from without—we reflect on what sight gives to us. In this sense, we have double vision. As Merleau-Ponty says, "Vision alone teaches us that beings that are different, 'exterior,' foreign to one another, are yet absolutely *together*, are 'simultaneity'."[11] So while we are aware of the fact that the image demonstrates the split between

---

**11** Maurice Merleau-Ponty, "Eye and Mind," *The Merleau-Ponty Reader*, eds. Ted Toadvine and Leonard Lawlor (Evanston, IL: Northwestern University Press, 2007), 375.

appearance and reality, we understand its curious congruence with the world, since it shimmers at the border of the real. When we encounter the visionary, or the intersection of the real with the unreal, what we think we know about seeing is, ultimately, challenged.

This intersecting moment, which exerts the same pressure as metaphor does, demands that we hold two perspectives in our minds at once. (In this sense, it is the same as the ekphrastic moment.) Because we don't find ourselves in the *Isenheim Altarpiece*, for instance, our distress comes from the knowledge that we *could* be wholly absent from the world. We *could* be gone from it. We can hold this thought only briefly in our minds, until the idea of not existing becomes too much for us to bear. In her discussion of *Las Meninas*, a painting by Diego Velasquez, Anne Carson says: "Arrest occurs ... at a blind point where the reality of what we are disappears into the possibility of what we could be if we were other than we are."[12]

Carson uses one powerful word when she speaks of arrest. She observes that it comes about when reality coincides with "possibility." Both the writer and the artist understand how things are, but they give us what might be. And, in fact, they are not shy about showing us how possibility works—that is, they lay bare the operation of a work of art, but allow us to go beyond it. We see the hand of the painter who paints, or the hand of the writer who writes. We are well aware of how disbelief has been suspended, but this

---

**12** Anne Carson, *Eros, the Bittersweet* (1986 rpt. Champaign, IL: Dalkey Archive Press, 1998), 75.

doesn't lessen our fascination. The *Isenheim Altarpiece*, for instance, gives us a mortal Christ—a corpse, stinking of disease—but it also gives us this same corpse transformed into an immortal Christ. And, of course, the implication for those looking at the painting in Grünewald's time would have been that whoever looked at the painting had the potential to be transformed too. Even now, we can appreciate this idea. We *could* be gone from the world when we look at the altarpiece, but the alternative is that we *could* be more than what we are—we could be changed, blazingly, into more radiant selves.

In my high-school geography class, the teacher gave us stereoscopic glasses and asked us to look at aerial photographs of a farming community near Flamborough, Ontario. We were given two nearly duplicate aerial photographs of the same scene, laid precisely beside each other. Seen through stereoscopic glasses, the two-dimensional aerial photographs abruptly became one, with the images springing into three dimensions—the fields contained hollows and hills, trees cast shadows on the ground below, and a brook snaked down a slope and disappeared into a culvert under a road. My depth perception had allowed me to see it, and I knew this, but it was as though I had been allowed to see how the rabbit emerged from the magician's hat.

This same magic, that of intersection, is what keeps us transfixed by a painting like the *Isenheim Altarpiece*. It transcends the elements that allow it to take shape—form, colour, and depth—in order to carry us out of our own time and place. One sight of the Virgin Mary dandling her infant on her knee shows us the picture of domestic bliss. One glance at this same mother beside her dead son is enough to convince us of the weight of grief. One look at the weirdly animated Christ zooming up from his broken grave mesmerizes us. We accept all such transformations. There is no question about the power exuded by the altarpiece. As Merleau-Ponty says, speaking of paintings: "it is [not] a matter of adding one dimension to the two of the canvas, of organizing an illusion ... [instead, it] is a spectacle of something ... by breaking the 'skin of things' to show how the things are made into things, how the world made world...."[13] It is true that, for me, the fact of seeing the figures of the altarpiece as if cut from the painting and set against the background of the Burlington Golf & Country Club allowed me to break the skin of things. I could only unsettle the familiar by examining what it was not. And so, by setting down something incongruous alongside it—something disruptive, but imaginative—by way of this vision of Grünewald's, I was able to regard both present and past in an entirely different way. This gesture, I began to see, was the gesture of metaphor.

⋆

As I was finishing this essay, a friend sent me some information about the *Keiskamma Altarpiece*, a huge work inspired by the *Isenheim*. It was made by 130 women and men of the Eastern Cape region in South Africa. Finished in 2005, it consists of embroidered panels that open to show other

---

**13** Maurice Merleau-Ponty, 370.

panels depicting the experience of those devastated by the AIDS/HIV epidemic. There is no Nativity in this altarpiece; instead, the first panel is the Crucifixion, showing a woman recently widowed, a clutch of orphans, and an old woman sitting on a bed. This set of panels opens to show a joyful Resurrection, in which trees are leafing into fullness, birds are winging through the air, and people are singing and dancing—all of it alive with whirling shapes and colours. The final panel shows the current reality of the Eastern Cape; it includes large photographs of the grandmothers who care for orphaned children.[14] As a vision arising out of suffering, it parallels the *Isenheim Altarpiece* poignantly. Both works of art emerge out of a response to disease, and both have to do with care of the sick. But, fundamentally, what the *Keiskamma Altarpiece* showed me is the communal nature of such art. It isn't simply meant for one or two people to see; it's meant for an entire community. Only in this way can people who have dealt with illness, and who have seen it all around them, imagine healing that restores not just a few, but many. And the vision enlarges us. Perhaps this enlargement of vision is what Merleau-Ponty meant when he spoke of art that breaks the skin of the world. It is through this kind of art that we are, all of us, participants in the possible.

---

**14** More information about the *Keiskamma Altarpiece* may be found at *www.keiskamma.org*.

November afternoon -
Isaac's Harbour

# *The Dark Side of Fiction's Moon*

In late November of 2006, I attended public hearings arranged by the province of Nova Scotia to review the environmental assessment of a proposed liquefied natural gas (LNG) project planned for the Goldboro area of Guysborough County, about fifty kilometres from Antigonish. The proposed project involved the construction of a large petrochemical complex, including a receiving terminal and storage facility for the liquefied natural gas, a cogeneration power plant, and a chemical processing facility. The chemical plant would convert ethane and propane into ethylene and propylene, with the aim of processing these further into polyethylene and polypropylene resin, or plastic pellets. These plastic pellets would be sold to manufacturers for use in making plastic products for consumers.

The area that would be taken up by this project would cover more than 200 hectares of land. A dam would have to be built at Meadow Lake to provide water to the facilities. A new road would have to be built, connecting Goldboro with Antigonish, because of the anticipated heavy truck traffic; it would cross several watercourses. A marginal wharf and marine terminal, extending into the waters of Isaac's Harbour, would have to be built to accommodate the tankers arriving from any of the twelve nations (many of which are politically troubled) with liquefaction facilities that export LNG, including Algeria, Brunei, Indonesia, Iran, Libya, Malaysia, Nigeria, Oman, Qatar, United Arab Emirates, and Trinidad and Tobago.

Not only did I think that such a project represented short-term thinking (especially given that natural gas isn't a renewable resource), I also suspected that the so-called environmental assessment, completed by the company, was a glossing-over of the facts. I'd read about the accidents that had occurred in the transportation of liquefied natural gas. I also knew that in the United States and Italy, protests against LNG terminals had been successful, since the populations in these countries were seen to be at risk.

But I decided to go to the hearings and listen to what people were saying; I'd be able to glean more information. The hearings were held in a conference room at the Greenway Claymore Inn. Along one side of the large room, a series of tables had been lined up, each covered in a white cloth and skirted with a blue one: behind these tables sat the experts hired by the company proposing the project. Anyone asking a question or making a comment had to walk to a microphone facing the front of the room, where two representatives from the Nova Scotia Environmental Assessment Board presided over the hearings.

One of the few who challenged the company's environmental assessment was Chantal Gagnon, from the Ecology Action Centre in Halifax. Occasionally, she was joined by others from the centre. Of the other speakers, most had particular, vested interests; one represented the County of Antigonish, and another the County of Guysborough. Several represented unions. Other than Chantal Gagnon and the staff members of the Ecology Action Centre, only a handful of people raised questions. Most of the speakers were interested in a project that would bring jobs to a region of the country where unemployment is high. From the beginning, I thought that the hearings were a mere formality and that the project would receive approval. For me, and perhaps for some others, there was a sense of anxiety, of dread, produced in that room—the sense of a foregone conclusion.

The quality of that disquiet was the same sense of unease I got when reading certain kinds of fiction. As I thought about it over a period of a few days, I realized that it was fiction involving the uncanny, or the *unheimlich*, as Freud calls it.[1] Within the word *unheimlich* is its root, *heimlich*, which connotes the intimacy of home, as well as that which is hidden or concealed. When Freud gives us the word *unheimlich*, he points out that whatever has been familiar, or known, in the way of being at home in one's own skin can be revealed as something alien.

---

1 Sigmund Freud, "The Uncanny," in *The Norton Anthology of Theory and Criticism*, eds. Vincent B. Letich et al. (New York: W.W. Norton, 2001), 929–952.

No stories or novels are as uncanny as those involving a double, or *doppelgänger*. Such fiction begins with the familiar, or original character, into whose domain intrudes the unfamiliar *doppelgänger*: one character is accepted as being true, but the other casts him into doubt. The double encapsulates a strangeness, or quality of the *unheimlich*, that feeds back into the original. In this way, the *doppelgänger* challenges meaning itself. Who are we, once we have been invaded, even sundered, by another, however unbelievable that other may be? The problem of identity in such fiction is never clearly resolved, nor is the issue of its relationship to the world it represents, if this fiction acts as a sort of *doppelgänger* to reality. Which world has more solidity—the outward one of reality or the inward one of imagination? All fiction seeks to be regarded as reality, but this becomes especially intriguing in tales involving the *doppelgänger*, since the very device of the double splits fiction's "reality" further.

We find ourselves looking into the work looking into itself, whether we are reading Robert Louis Stevenson's *The Strange Case of Dr. Jeykll and Mr. Hyde*, Edgar Allan Poe's *William Wilson*, Oscar Wilde's *The Picture of Dorian Gray*, Fyodor Dostoevsky's *The Double*, Vladimir Nabokov's *Despair*, or a recent novel, also named *The Double*, by José Saramago. All unlock, in various ways, the Pandora's box of the self, with some characters meeting a desperate end, whether by the knifing of a portrait (which results in the death of the character who wields the knife), as in *The Picture of Dorian Gray*, or by the stabbing of an evil double, as in *William Wilson*. The protagonist realizes, though by then it is too late, that he or she contains more than a single self. Fiction doesn't just allow for such fecundity, it embraces it, exploring proliferations because it is generative. But fiction involving a double generates dread: almost at once we sense that no good can come of it.

⊰⊰•⊱⊱

In Dostoevsky's novel *The Double*, Golyadkin is aware of a change from his first view of his reflection in the mirror one morning. He wonders whether something might be wrong, but immediately convinces himself that all is well. Of course all is not well, and this becomes clear during his exchange with the doctor, Krestyan Ivanovitch. Golyadkin is told to expect not only a radical change in his life, but a break in his character. His first view of his double occurs by the Fontanka Embankment in the midst of a snowstorm. Disturbed, he runs toward home, followed by a lost dog, but the stranger races there too, and gets there before him. By the end of the short novel, the original Golyadkin is so undone that, as he endures a kiss from the confident, efficient double who has replaced him, he senses that Olsufy Ivanovitch's house is filled with a multitude of Golyadkins. And when he is hustled away in a carriage, even the doctor is transformed, gazing at him with the burning eyes of a demon. The strange, flickering brilliance of Dostoevsky's *The Double* is that the madness of the world is realized so dramatically through the eyes of a man who is himself descending into madness.

With his past and future taken away from him, he becomes nothing more than a wraith. His predicament condemns him to a living death.

Vladimir Nabokov's novel *Despair* points to the past by making references to fiction by Hesse, Gogol, and particularly Dostoevsky (sometimes the comments are wonderfully snide), and it, too, is an elegant study of a character's disintegration. Throughout the book, Nabokov plays with the question of whether the author of the novel is the main character, Hermann, or whether it is Nabokov himself. Referring to its own operations, the novel comments on itself as it moves forward, circles back, questions something, corrects it, and takes up the story again. As Nabokov points out in his autobiography, *Speak, Memory*: "In a first-rate piece of fiction, the real clash is not between the characters, but between the author and the world."[2] In exposing Hermann, Nabokov raises the question of whether the authentic self is the one watching, or the one watched; or, perhaps more pertinently, whether the self is the one who destroys, or the one destroyed. Hermann has discovered his double in a man called Felix, who is poor and uncouth, but whose name means "the happy one." Later, he devises a plan by which he will murder Felix, but appear to murder himself, in order to take on the dead man's identity.

The double presents a challenge to the self—a challenge that needs to be sustained, or somehow held in suspense, if it

---

**2** Vladimir Nabokov, *Speak, Memory: An Autobiography Revisited* (1947, rpt. London: Weidenfeld and Nicolson, 1967), 290.

is to be successful. But the double is disturbing, even terrifying. In Dostoevsky's *The Double,* for instance, Golyadkin is shattered by the appearance of his double:

> ... he was trembling all over. His knees turned to jelly, and with a groan he sat down.... There was indeed cause for alarm, for he thought there was something familiar about the stranger ... he was now almost sure it was someone he knew. He'd seen him often. He'd seen him somewhere quite recently even. But where?[3]

Whenever a *doppelgänger* appears in fiction, the sight of him—with a face so weirdly like the protagonist's own—has a powerful effect that seems to detonate the narrative. In *Despair,* Hermann is taken aback when he comes across a sleeping tramp, Felix, while walking in the country outside Prague on a fresh, spring day, but it is only later that he feels completely undone by the encounter: "I doubted the reality of what I saw, doubted my own sanity, felt sick and faint—honestly I was forced to sit down, my knees were shaking so."[4]

In both novels, the strange figure of the double remains at a distance, even when he comes close. He is both near and far, simultaneously; appearing, retreating and appearing again, and he retains his mystery by keeping his distance. But what sort of identity is the protagonist left with, once he has been unsettled by this encounter and its consequences?

---

**3** Fyodor Dostoevsky, *The Double: A Poem of St. Petersburg,* trans. George Bird (1866, rpt. London: The Harvill Press, 1957), 78. **4** Nabokov, *Despair* (1936, rpt. London: Weidenfeld & Nicolson, 1966), 17.

As the philosopher Emmanuel Levinas puts it: "the Stranger ... disturbs the being [or the one] at home with oneself.... But Stranger also means free one. Over him I have no *power*."[5] As Dostoevsky's novel progresses, for instance, we see that Golyadkin has no power over the strange man who calmly inserts himself into Golyadkin's life, and seems to know, with more certainty than Golyadkin himself, how to move confidently within this social milieu. As Levinas suggests, it seems to be exactly such a stranger who "puts the I in question."[6] This calling into question heralds a disruption in the complacency of the self.

⟵•⟶

"Give your name, please," said the man seated at the front of the room.

"Pardon?" I said.

"Your name—we need to record it." The man spoke in a way that was not unkindly. The hearings had been going on for days, and he seemed weary.

I gave my name; it was duly recorded.

"Thank you. Start again, please."

I was keenly aware that the room was not arranged for dialogue. The moment I went up to the microphone and started speaking, I was pegged as an adversary. It unsettled me; my hands were clammy and my mouth was dry. David Suzuki says that in the environmental battles he has seen,

---

**5** Emmanuel Levinas, *Totality and Infinity: An Essay on Exteriority*, trans. Alphonso Lingis (1961, rpt. Pittsburgh, PA: Duquesne University Press, 1969), 39. **6** Ibid, 195.

or participated in, since the sixties, "one side is invariably pitted against the other ... [and] I realized we had to find common ground. We couldn't go on skirmishing over the planet...."[7] But in that room in the Greenway Claymore Inn we seemed to be continuing the skirmish.

I asked a question about how the Black Loyalist burial ground at Red Head would be affected by the construction of the project. It wasn't a question I'd researched; I was following up on something Chantal Gagnon had mentioned earlier. Those who answered the question assured me that the remains of the Black Loyalists had been removed to a nearby cemetery because of the erosion of Red Head. Still, I countered, it had been a burial ground of special historical significance to the province.

What I said wasn't very persuasive, but after I sat down I realized I could still make a stand on behalf of the land. At the very least I could go to Red Head and write about it.

I began attending to those who stood for the interests of the "proponent." None of the experts seated behind the tables *wanted* to do harm; they weren't against the land, despite the fact that exploitation of its non-renewable resources couldn't be achieved without harm. As I looked at them, it was as if I saw my own face in the faces of those around me.

---

**7** David Suzuki with Amanda McConnell, *The Sacred Balance: Rediscovering Our Place in Nature* (Vancouver, BC: Greystone Books, 1997), unpaginated preface.

The *doppelgänger* is certainly a stranger, one whose entrance alarms the protagonist, but can it really be said that this figure resembles Levinas's vision of the Other? It may be useful to look at Levinas's notions of Same (or self) and Other more closely. Levinas tells us that the Other is infinitely mysterious, one who withdraws from sight and touch. This notion of the Other seems curiously disembodied, until we recall Yahweh of the Old Testament, who is present to the Israelites only as a speaker, one who *is* word or Logos.

And, since the Other is infinite, it takes precedence, coming in advance of the self in order to situate otherness within it. This bifurcation of the self by the Other comes *before* all else—before being, action, and freedom. Because of this, the Other gives the self its particular and unique identity, yet this identity is always an identity that is in-relation-to, or responsible-for, the Other. It is, Levinas says, because we have a sense of such otherness already within us that we can't neglect the stranger in our midst. The summons of the Other is ignored at the peril of each individual, since we are called upon to respond.

Levinas gives the Other a face, but observes that the particularities of a face, or its features, are not what gives it significance. What gives the face importance is that it issues a demand—that of an ethical response from us: "the face is exposed, menaced, as if inviting us to an act of violence. At the same time, the face is what forbids us to kill."[8] In other words, the face exceeds whatever we take to mean "face." Instead of simply being a feature of the body, the

---

**8** Levinas, *Ethics and Infinity: Conversations with Philippe Nemo,* trans. Richard A. Cohen (1982, rpt. Pittsburgh, PA: Duquesne University Press, 1985), 86.

face inquires into the onlooker's motives at the same time as it appeals to his or her conscience. As Levinas says, "[t]he face speaks."[9] And yet the face remains beyond perception. Levinas reveals that the face is not what we take it to be, since it is not mere flesh.

But we can't prevent the picture of a face coming to mind when we consider the Other, even as we try to stop ourselves. Levinas eliminates the corporeality, particularly the face, of the Other, "freeing it from the image that it is forever tempted to lapse into."[10] This explains why he says the face is invisible. So long as it is tangible, it can be reduced to a thing. But it threatens, time and again, to burst the restrictions placed upon it—a face is deeply compelling, whether in reality, or as an image. W.J.T. Mitchell says that the image of the face has a powerful, deeply felt hold over us. He relates an anecdote about Roland Barthes, who, coming across a photograph of his mother in a winter garden, could not shake its almost magical grip upon him.[11] So by mentioning the face and then erasing it, Levinas ensures, paradoxically, that the face becomes hauntingly present.

Too much is at stake for the Other to be wholly disclosed, which is why Levinas doesn't want us to depend upon sight. The Other must remain hidden, since, coming into view, it would become finite. If we could see or know the Other, we would be able to resist, violate, or kill such a presence. A body is exposed to the world, making it vulnerable. It

---

**9** Levinas, *Totality and Infinity*, 66. **10** Philippe Crignon, Nicole Simek, and Zahi Zalloua, "Figuration: Emmanuel Levinas and the Image," *Yale French Studies*, No. 104, Encounters with Levinas (2004), 100–125. **11** W.J.T. Mitchell, *What Do Pictures Want? The Lives and Loves of Images* (Chicago, IL: University of Chicago Press, 2005), 9.

also has the potential to be duplicated as an image, and to become common rather than rare. The divinity that takes on flesh runs the risk of diminishment—no wonder prohibitions regarding image-making of deities were frequently imposed. For instance, the second commandment of the Bible, banning graven images, shows how well people understood the nature of art, with its potential for unlimited replication and proliferation. It's a dangerous thing to reveal the godhead.

So the infinite Other can't come into view without being reduced. But how do we have a sense of the Other, if the Other lacks a body and a place in the world? Levinas has a solution: "the dimension of the divine opens forth from the human face."[12] The Other holds itself in reserve, but we sense it in the face of the other person. And this person is the stranger, widow, or orphan. Still, the stranger, widow, and orphan are all somewhat nebulous abstractions who remain faceless. It's left to fiction to conjure up the vision. But the *doppelgänger* doesn't fit the Levinasian idea of the Other. He doesn't reveal "the dimension of the divine" in his face; on the contrary, he inspires fear, precisely because he appears as a mirror image. He resembles.

But the deeper issue is that the double appears to be both self and one who is radically different from self. The double's disquieting ability to mimic is terrifying at first because of the extent to which he resembles, but as events proceed, it's not this that distresses the protagonist—it's

---

**12** Levinas, *Totality and Infinity*, 78.

that while resembling, he differs. So mimesis is not simply a way to effect sameness, but also to split it open. The double is relentless. By appearing to be same-as, but by being different-from, the double holds the protagonist in an ongoing arrest so long as he appears in the work of fiction. And the protagonist is required to face things. Whatever he does in response, he's always exposed: there is no shelter.

So one character longs to destroy the other, or at least to undermine him—anything to break the spell. In Nabokov's *Despair,* for instance, Hermann meets with Felix to get him to agree to a scheme in which Felix, unknowingly, will aid in his own demise. But Felix regards Hermann dubiously: "And what if it's all a lie?...What if I don't believe you?"[13] In the end, Hermann gets Felix to go along with it. He's thought of everything to ensure that things go smoothly, giving Felix a shave and a pedicure, and even going so far as to clip a few hairs from his eyebrows. Before he shoots Felix in the back, he gives him his good clothes to wear, so that when he falls in the snow, it seems to be none other than Hermann Karlovich who's been brutally killed. He gazes at the body with avid interest:

> There are mysterious moments and that was one of them. Like an author reading his work over a thousand times, probing and testing every syllable, and finally unable to say of this brindle of words whether it is good or not, so it happened with me.... But there is the maker's secret certainty, which can never err.... I could not say who had been killed, I or he.

---

**13** Nabokov, *Despair,* 106.

> And while I looked, it grew dark in the vibrating wood, and with that face before me slowly dissolving, vibrating fainter and fainter, it seemed as if I were looking at my image in a stagnant pool.[14]

What has Hermann done? He has made something, with a "maker's secret certainty," but his making is murder. He refers to this work as his masterpiece, but later, as he writes

---

**14** Ibid, 181–182.

Red Head, Isaac's Harbour (site of former Black Loyalist burial grounds)

an account of events and realizes that he has made a mistake, he revises his view of his marvellous work: on the first page of his manuscript he scrawls a title, *Despair,* the same title as the book by Nabokov. In the here and now, however, he has achieved his goal—Felix is dead. The pale face of the corpse becomes Hermann's own face dissolving in a rank, dark pool as if it were floating. It is the hour of shadows and dreams: a twilit half-world, from which Hermann will emerge not as himself, but as a phantom. He becomes Felix, but he can't become Felix: still, he is about to try to begin living the life of a man who is dead. Here the narrative is ruptured. The novel becomes more agitated, even nervous, just as the protagonist begins to retreat, in an irritated way, into his distrust of the human race. Was there ever a Hermann, or a Felix? Already identity has been questioned through the device of the double; now, with the killing of the double, the very reality of those characters—their subjectivity—is in question. So the reader is drawn into the unworlding of a world.

⁂

Not long ago, I drove from Antigonish to Isaac's Harbour on a sunny November day. I wanted to walk there and get a sense of the land. I imagined that fences might have been erected around the site proposed for the liquefied natural gas complex, but nothing had been done, except that a portion of the area had been zoned "Heavy Industrial." Still, much had changed in the long period of time since the hearings. The recent financial crisis meant the price of natural gas had fallen; this might have put the project on hold.

I stopped north of Goldboro, at Stormont, and made my way along the Loyalists' Trail, a path several kilometres in length that runs from Stormont southwest to the water's edge at the shingle of Leggett Point, where, inside a shed, I found information about the unfortunate Loyalists. The rough land over which I'd walked was impossible to farm, but it had been parcelled out to a contingent of these settlers, many of whom had fought for the British in the American

Revolution. There were blacks among them, some of whom were free blacks, and some who were listed as servants. In the late autumn of 1783, they had sailed from Florida, a territory that had been relinquished by Britain (to Spain). So these Loyalists left Florida in autumn, a season of gales. They arrived in northern Nova Scotia in the bitter cold of December, when they had to build makeshift shelters in difficult conditions. Many simply covered their huts with roofs of brush. This would have kept out the snow, but when the spring rains assailed them the huts must have been wet as well as cold. It's a mystery how any of the 900 people could have survived the winter on a frozen snout of land between Isaac's Harbour and Country Harbour. In conditions of great deprivation, a third of them sickened (mainly because of scurvy) and died. I went out of the shed, and saw that the cure for the disease was nearby, had they only known. The bark of the white spruce, and the scarlet rosehips still clinging to the wild rose bushes, could be put into boiling water and made into a drink rich in vitamin C.

There were no signs of habitation near the Loyalists' Trail now: this was sparsely populated country. The trail was strewn with small rocks and boulders, and the ground was hummocky. The mosses were rich and various, with peat moss lining the side of the path in several spots. When I picked up a clump and squeezed it, water poured to the ground as if I were clutching a sponge. I found feather moss, one of my favourites, which is like the feathery back of a bird. And hidden in the moss, I could see goldthread; its yellow roots—or gold threads—dangled from my fingers when I plucked them free of the moss. The place where I was kneeling was dappled with sunlight, and the mosses were bright green even in the shadows.

I left this mossy nook reluctantly, and walked to the car, looking at the map again before setting out. I wasn't quite sure where Red Head was located. I drove several kilometres south to Drum Head, where, from the wharf, I had a good view of a drumlin that stuck out of the water like half a head; I could see how erosion had taken away one side of it. Could this be Red Head? I had driven right past it. I doubled back and drove slowly along the harbour toward Goldboro, parked the car at the edge of the road and walked down a driveway, past a barn and a tidy white house. Even though my map wasn't detailed, it showed that this was the only piece of land jutting out into Isaac's Harbour; presumably, this was the area designated for the marginal wharf for the petrochemical complex.

Near a tidal pool close to the shore, a man was picking bog cranberries. He had grown up in the area, and the tidy white house belonged to his aunt. Pointing in the direction of the half-headed drumlin, which was now much nearer, he said that it had been the burial ground of Black Loyalists. So it was indeed Red Head. I thanked the man and made my way to it along a stony crescent of beach, the northwest wind cutting against the side of my face. The headland was linked to the shore by this beach; I came across another small tidal pool, fringed with heather, below the slope. When I crested the top of Red Head, the wind was strong, and I was grateful for my gloves and earmuffs. I could see where bodies had been exhumed, no doubt from unmarked graves. There were shallow indentations in the soil, and I recalled a photograph I'd seen of people on this site in 2001, when the remains had been dug up and removed to alleviate the danger of losing them as the land crumbled into Isaac's Harbour. But when bones have been moved, can we say that the earth that held them no longer contains anything of those people? When I climbed past the fence of spruce trees to the top of Red Head and looked out over the dark blue water, I knew that this site had been chosen for a reason. It was a high place, between sky and water. Perhaps some places are sacred: if so, this crown of land was one of them, even as it eroded.

On my way back to the car I passed the man who'd been picking cranberries; he was still picking them, but he'd moved farther inland. He explained that the company no longer intended to build the wharf on Red Head, but a little farther southeast. He wore a T-shirt, thin jacket, and jeans tucked into rubber boots; in his belt was a hunting knife. His eyes were kindly, but he looked away when he said that things would all change soon enough. I could see what he meant. It didn't matter where the wharf was built; the nature and scope of the project was such that it would change everything. The land wouldn't be the same, nor would the ocean—soon enough would come the unworlding of a world.

⁂

Sometimes there is a rift in fiction where it withdraws from its own invention, where it stands apart from what has been created. And it is at this point that we sense something nocturnal in the work. In *Despair*, after the murder of Felix, Hermann is still very much alive, straining to keep one step ahead of those who might have discovered his mistake. He is his own worst enemy. And there is no exit, since the gendarme will find him. Even the sentences give us no escape: "Abominably cold. Dogs barking: one of them begins and then all the others join in. It is raining. The electric lights are wan, yellow. What on earth have I done?"[15] Shortly after this, Hermann gazes out his window at the people who crowd around the house where he has taken a room, waiting for him to be brought to justice. He wonders if his existence is unreal, and whether everything he has done has been a dream.

But it isn't a dream. As Levinas puts it: "to kill, like to die, is to seek an escape from being, to go where freedom and negation operate. Horror is the event of being which returns in the heart of this negation, as though nothing had happened."[16] It is not the anxiety about the destruction of one's being that brings about this sense of dread. It is not caused by a fear of dying. Instead, it is exposure to that which is incessant, trapping us so we are unable to escape. It is the materiality of this incessancy that is frightening to us, as if it were a constant buzzing in our ears: "There is nothing, but there is being, like a field of forces."[17] The vague "something" is sinister because it is, apparently, there, even

**15** Nabokov, *Despair*, 220. **16** Levinas, "There is: Existence without Existents" in *The Levinas Reader*, ed. Seán Hand (London: Basil Blackwell, 1989), 33. **17** Ibid, 35.

if it can't be seen. Lacking subjectivity and substantiality, this force field, Levinas says, constitutes the *il y a*— "like a density of the void, like a murmur of silence ... a presence of absence."[18] And this presence-in-absence remains disquieting. There is no relief from it, just as there is no end to sleeplessness for an insomniac.

As Levinas clarifies his notion of the *il y a*, he turns to literature. He offers the poetry of Rimbaud, and the work of Blanchot, Huysmans, Racine, de Maupassant, and Zola. He discusses the shades of Shakespeare, particularly the ghost of Banquo in *Macbeth*, which is "a decisive experience of the 'no exit' from existence, its phantom return through the fissures through which one has driven it."[19] To be in this predicament, in which passage or movement is interrupted, is to be suspended in a night that continues through the day.

Those in extreme situations, hovering in the borderland between insanity and lucidity, know its terrors. Golyadkin is a good example. He realizes the impossibility of his escape at the end of Dostoevsky's *The Double*, when the weirdly inhuman Dr. Rutenspitz appears: "The door flew open with a bang, and on the threshold stood a man whose very appearance made Mr. Golyadkin's blood run cold.... His eyes froze Mr. Golyadkin with horror. With a grave, solemn visage, this terrible man approached the sorry hero of our tale."[20] Golyadkin can't cry out or run away: this is what he's been dreading all along.

Nowhere is the notion of the *il y a* more powerfully realized than in fiction that involves the double. Such fiction

---

**18** Ibid, 35. **19** Ibid, 33. **20** Dostoevsky, *The Double*, 250.

involves a confrontation with self and another being that is deeply disconcerting, and, finally, devastating, because it is a challenge to the very thing that appears most familiar. Yet it is through the struggle between the self and the double, often a struggle to the death, that we sense the *il y a*. The double makes the self into an outcast and sets it to wandering. The world becomes a place of terrors, not a place of comfort, where the self is no more unique than a speck of dust. If the *il y a* were to take a living, breathing shape, it might take the shape of the double, the embodiment of that which cares not for the self.

Could it be that Levinas's notions of the Other and the *il y a* are not so far apart after all? Is there a place where they elide into one another? Levinas points to something interesting when he says that "the Other is not only an alter ego: the Other is what I myself am not."[21] He suggests that the Other is open and limitless: an alternative to the enclosed self. But it isn't certain whether the Other is a being at all, for the Other is what I myself am not. The Other is "absolutely different from any possible conception of it based on experience ... unlike even what one takes it to be, namely, a 'person' with all the essential properties and existential qualities one deems a person to have."[22] Levinas is pointing us in the direction of the Other, but he could be describing the *il y a*, which is certainly what I myself am not.

Others have noticed that the Levinasian Other may be

---

**21** Levinas, "Time and the Other," in *The Levinas Reader,* ed. Seán Hand (London: Basil Blackwell, 1989), 48. **22** Benjamin Hutchens, *Levinas: A Guide for the Perplexed* (London: Continuum, 2004), 21.

regarded in more than one way. Simon Critchley asks, "is it not in the excessive experience of evil and horror … that the ethical subject first assumes its shape? Does this not begin to explain why the royal road to ethical metaphysics must begin by making Levinas a master of the literature of horror? But if this is the case, why is radical otherness goodness? Why is alterity ethical?"[23] It's true that even as we see the validity of the argument Levinas brings to bear, that of responsibility to others, his vision of alterity may, ultimately, leave us in the dust. It is a vision that moves so far beyond the human that it can't help but disturb us. At its furthest edge, it leaves us with the sense that the Other may be inhuman, that even goodness may be inhuman. Levinas might have countered this by saying that where the Other allows for boundless possibility, the *il y a* does not. It imprisons. And it is boundless in oppression, infinite in its incessancy. But Critchley's questions remain; there is a nagging sense that the Other might be capable of terrorizing us.

Literature makes a movement towards the *il y a* out of necessity, since its work is to press against the boundaries of subjectivity and the erasure of subjectivity, or the very limits of the human. Inevitably, the work of the imagination makes its way to the place from which everything has departed. In an almost impossible gesture, it resists what it confronts, without shelter, uncertainly facing the possibility of a world without others. It will fail in the attempt, but

---

**23** Simon Critchley, *Very Little … Almost Nothing: Death, Philosophy, Literature* (London: Routledge, 1997), 80.

go there it must, employing a language that is broken by interruptions or gaps, words that stutter into incoherence. Why does it go there at all? And why is it concerned with a time that seems only an interruption of time, a stalling of the usual progress of time? It goes there because it makes the attempt to give us that which is almost beyond imagining, in order to try and disclose it. Already exiled, it goes further into its own exile, moving into the territory that lies on the hither side of the known. Its work consists of showing us "a rifting of earth and world that holds open the opening of the world in a constant condition of exposure to the non-identical."[24] It shows us a time beyond time, a place beyond place, as only art can do. It gives us glimpses of otherness, whether these glimpses are uplifting or not. As a contemporary and friend of Levinas, the writer Maurice Blanchot says, "in the world of beings that exist and of things that subsist there comes, as presence, not another world but the other of all worlds: not a possible world but an impossibility that estranges the world from itself."[25]

It goes through this estrangement to take up a position of witness outside the world we know. Literature is outside the economy, outside society, outside history. And just as the double casts the self into an inhospitable place, so fiction takes the reader there. There may not be a way out, but it is not the work of literature to ensure safe passage.

---

**24** Gerald L. Bruns, *Maurice Blanchot: The Refusal of Philosophy* (Baltimore, MD: The Johns Hopkins University Press), 85. **25** Blanchot, ibid, 85.

If the *il y a* were to take on a human shape, it could be embodied as the double, as I've said. But if the *il y a* could be imagined as landscape, it might be Isaac's Harbour rebuilt as a petrochemical complex. If the project goes ahead, this landscape will be scoured and remade into one that serves mere usefulness; in this sense, it will have been colonized. Such landscapes are notable for their sameness. But in fifty or sixty years, when the natural gas reserves are exhausted, the petrochemical complex will have no more use; it will have reached its natural termination. At this point, it may be abandoned, or in the jargon used at the environmental assessment hearings, it will have to be decommissioned. Imagine, then, what this place might look like, with a huge, disused marine wharf built for supertankers, old storage facilities for liquefied natural gas standing on polluted soil, a power generation plant that no longer operates, a chemical plant that has released a multiplicity of toxins into the air, earth, and water. By then, the lobster and mussel habitats may have been entirely compromised, while harbour waters may have been contaminated.

Certainly the uniqueness of this landscape will have been erased. It will not simply be a landscape of sameness, since, if sameness were to be enlarged, it would become something worse. So this landscape might have the look of a place estranged from itself—turned away from itself—and transformed into a world that perhaps Levinas only guessed at when he first introduced his notion of the *il y a*. It might show us our utter homelessness in a place where we once thought home could be.

But none of it may come to pass.

I got in the car and started up the road, taking one last look at the wide expanse of Isaac's Harbour as I went. From one point I could see all the way down the long harbour toward the ocean—a spectacular unrolling of blue, deep blue, deepest blue. I didn't want to forget any of it.

# *World at Play*

When I arrived at the Elizabeth Bishop House in Great Village, Nova Scotia, it was in the cool of late spring, and the yellow tulips were incandescent among the garden's greenery. The red tulips, lip-smackingly scarlet, were looking a little worse for wear, some with drooping petals. In the days before, it had been raining—the hard, driving rain had flattened some parts of the garden. But on the morning I arrived, the sun had come out: it was bright, and I couldn't bear to be inside. I sat on the porch, coffee in hand.

I was staying, for the second time, in the childhood home of Elizabeth Bishop, the Pulitzer-prize-winning American poet. Born in Worcester, Massachusetts, in 1911, her roots were Canadian; she was imaginatively bound to Nova Scotia, where she spent several of her childhood years with her grandparents. The modest clapboard farmhouse, with a small plaque designating it as a provincial heritage house, once belonged to Elizabeth Bishop's grandparents, the Bulmers (variously known as the Boomers). It was the same house to which Bishop returned again and again, in poetry and prose, to vivify her sharply felt experiences for her readers.

It is now a writers' retreat, co-owned by a group of Canadians and Americans. The fact that it has become a house for writers is due, chiefly, to the time and effort devoted to it by Sandra Barry, who oversees the comings and goings of the writers who stay here. She is herself a writer and independent scholar, one who has spent much of her time researching and writing about the life and work of Elizabeth Bishop. I had arranged with Sandra to spend five days at the house, a place where I felt very much at home.

But it was too inviting a day to sit for long; I took the mug inside and put it in the sink. Walking down the road to the southeast, I went over the bridge and up the hill to the cenotaph, past the tiny convenience store (with Jumbo Hot Dogs, New Movies Every Week, and Pizza Specials / Pizza by the Slice), the old post office, in a building not much bigger than a postage stamp, and along the road to the Great Village Elementary School. At the Wharf Road, marked by the stately old Blaikie House, which had been transformed into a bed and breakfast, I turned right. I knew the road already, having gone on walks there the previous November. The road led over the Great Village River, and away from it, up and over a hill, with cows staring at me like somber judges, although there was one with a rueful, I've-been-at-the-bar-a-little-too-long expression. I laughed; the cow didn't blink. At the top of the hill was a yellow house surrounded by a white fence, and beyond it, a long sloping path down to the shore with its leathery mud, overlaid with what seemed to be strips of silk— the pale blue water of

Cobequid Bay, which flows into the Minas Basin, becoming part of the Fundy.

I was thinking about the quality of play in Bishop's poetry. Her work is complex, and so avoids superficiality; something profoundly evocative lies beneath the apparently simple surface. In one of her poems, "Sestina," the clarity of objects, seen in their generous, almost delightful domesticity, give rise to what is not seen—something poignantly *missing*—to which the poem merely alludes. It isn't a poem about domestic bliss, but it's still playful. There's a sense of looking through a peephole at a miniature tableau: the doll-sized grandmother in her rocking chair, with combs in her silvery hair and slippers on her feet, the toy-like black stove and singing teakettle, and the child, perhaps with a sailor collar over her blouse, quietly drawing at the table. There is no father, no mother, only a man on the winding path of the child's picture. The little scene is slightly askew, but seems brightly coloured, making the sorrows that go unspoken all the more haunting.

I walked down the slope as far as the dyke that ran along the shore of the Cobequid. The dyke was no doubt originally built by Acadians (probably first built by the Robichaud family, who settled along the Wharf Road in 1720—as a helpful sign explains). It was like a high, grass-covered wall, and so kept out the wind as well as the salt water. But I couldn't see past it to the calm vista of the bay. To do that, I had to climb up and walk along the ridge at the top, tangled with brambles and grasses. I dropped back down to

the track below, lined with dandelions, and looked north, across the fields where a marsh hawk flew, level with the ground, towards the black spire of the church arrowing into the massing rain clouds above the jumble of Great Village. I couldn't see the gas station, but I knew it was there, radio blaring. To regard the village from a distance was to see it differently. I could have held it in the palm of my hand, nestled there with its greening maples and birches; pin cherries, newly flowering; ink-dark spruces, and, beyond, the rolling, blue Cobequid hills, which form a sort of postscript to

Mahon Cemetery, Great Village

the Appalachian Range. They were touched here and there with broad shafts of light.

I could have flicked the lightning rod on the steeple of the church with my fingernail, just as Bishop says in her prose piece, "In the Village."[1] How strange, yet oddly reassuring, to be part of the place she describes in her stories and poems: it was as though I'd been plunked down inside her imagination.

⊰⊷•⊶⊱

I returned to the Elizabeth Bishop House by way of a path that skirted a new cedar-shingled house, but to get to the main road I had to pass through a clear-cut. It looked like a battlefield, with some tree trunks upended and scattered, branches strewn every which way, and one or two trees left standing, like startled sentries. Too much Nova Scotian woodland had been logged, and was still being logged, in this way, because it is relatively cheap and easy; only a tiny fraction of old Acadian forest remains in the entire province. I passed through the clear-cut as quickly as I could, coming upon the Mahon Cemetery, where I found the gravestones for members of the Bulmer family. But the sky was clouding over and it looked like rain, so I headed to the road.

While I was walking down the hill to the village, trying

---

1 Bishop, "In the Village," *The Collected Prose* (New York: Farrar, Straus and Giroux, 1984), 251.

to stay on the narrow shoulder of the road to avoid the speedy traffic, it occurred to me that Bishop indulges in play while being conversant with, and mindful of, poetic form. Her work is as rigorous as it is playful, deeply engaged as it is freewheeling: this dichotomy sharpens our understanding of it. Her rigour appears to have been hard-won, from all accounts. She was not a prolific writer. Perhaps this was why she was strong-minded in her views about the teaching of creative writing, especially for children: "it's true, children sometimes write wonderful things, paint wonderful pictures, but I think they should be *dis*couraged."[2] This remark had a context. Though Bishop herself taught students at Harvard, she implied that the surfeit of poetry being produced in creative writing courses in the 1970s may have been the result of writers being too much encouraged.

By the time I got back to the house, it had begun to rain. It was cold inside, and I turned up the furnace and then, in the kitchen, began chopping vegetables for soup. By this time, there was a rushing sound of rain outside; it would soon be evening, but the sky was already dark. Once the soup had boiled, filling the small house with the aroma of carrots, onions, lentils and red peppers, I turned the burner down and went into the front room, sliding off my slippers to sit in a wicker chair. I picked up a book to read Bishop's "Sestina" again. Set in the kitchen where I had just been working, the poem had a surreal immediacy. Despite the

---

**2** Bishop, "The Art of Poetry," an interview with Elizabeth Spires in *The Paris Review Interviews,* Vol. I (1981, rpt., New York: Picador, 2006), 287.

fact that the present-day wood stove was not a Marvel but a grandmotherly Enterprise, or the fact that my pot of soup was simmering on an electric stove nearby, the scene of the poem was easy to imagine.

While the grandmother in "Sestina" is drinking tea that is full of tears, the child draws "a rigid house" with "a winding pathway."[3] I thought of a child busily working at a kitchen table while her grandmother puts the kettle on to boil. Twilight. Rain traces the glass of the windows as the kettle begins to sing. A pervasive sadness. And so the child draws a house and a man on the path with "buttons like tears" and shows it to her grandmother. Surely the grandmother praises the child's drawing, as the velvety glove of darkness envelopes the house and rain pelts against the windows. The grandmother settles back in her rocker, finishes her tea, and sings Baptist hymns in the general direction of the stove; the child draws another house. And the almanac, hanging by its string above the child in the kitchen, drops moons "like tears," as if sadness was seeded in that season, with summer gone and winter on its way.

After reading the poem, I got up and went back to the kitchen. On a shelf of the microwave stand, sure enough, there was a copy of *The Old Farmer's Almanac, 2006*. I flipped through it and found the tiny moons for the month of September. For each day of the month, I could locate the time of sunrise and sunset, moonrise and moonset, low tide and high tide (for Boston). The feast day of Saint Omer fell

---

**3** Bishop, "Sestina," *The Complete Poems, 1927–1979* (New York: The Noonday Press, Farrar, Straus and Giroux, 1983), 123.

on the same day—September 9th—that "Canadian swimmer Marilyn Bell became the first person to swim across Lake Ontario, 1954." In a column on the right-hand side, there was a pithy saying: "They tell you that cutting your firewood warms you twice." And there was a folksy rhyme for the month: "Hurricane threat, we bet. Up north, it's wet. Cool and dry and providential, then potentially torrential! Raincoats are essential!"[4] The almanac, a pocket-sized magazine, was made with a hole through its upper left corner so it could be tied with string and hung in a hall or kitchen. I thought of how it would hang, pages open: how things might seem to fall out of it. Not seeds, but tears. And what would the seed-tears fall into but air?

Bishop seems to have been a writer who worked with what was at hand, like someone tossing chopped vegetables into soup. But she was clear-sighted about her work, even as a young writer. In the summer after she graduated from Vassar College, returning to New York in the wake of a vacation at Cuttyhunk Island in Massachusetts, she made a valiant effort to get to work on writing poems. Scribbling notes for herself in the New York Public Library late in the summer of 1934, she wrote that poetry "proceeds from the material, the material eaten out with acid, pulled down from underneath, made to perform and always kept in order, in its

---

**4** Janice Stillman, ed. *The Old Farmer's Almanac, 2006* (Dublin, NH: Yankee Publishing Inc., 2006), 117.

place. Sometimes it cannot be made to indicate its spiritual goal clearly … but even then the spiritual must be felt."[5] The observation is exact. Bishop goes through *things* to try to locate the ineffable. Beyond the things she examines there is something else at stake, both hidden and compelling—it's this that enlarges her poetry.

This can be seen clearly in the way she made her small works of art, however much she might have suggested they were mere trifles. In an undated collage piece called *Anjinhos* (*Angels*), she arranged a surface that is partly covered with perfect faces of girls, some of whom are blonde and some brunette, each with a collar of golden wings.[6] These could be stamps for stationery, or simply a decorative paper ornament. Bishop defaced some of the angels with glitter, or perhaps glue and sand, so they look as though they are litter on a beach. There is a girl's crude wooden sandal at the bottom of the collage, and two butterflies—a blue one resembling a Blue Morpho at the top left, and a small yellow one. A baby's soother, painted black, a bottle cap, a butt of a cigarette, part of a ticket, a shell.

It is a curiously beautiful piece of work. It brings Joseph Cornell to mind: an artist whose work was much admired by Bishop. Her *Anjinhos,* in its light-blue shadow box, is its own poem, inspired by the drowning of a young girl in Rio de Janeiro. It is evidence of Bishop's practice of materiality. The poorly made sandal which could only have fit

---

**5** Bishop, in *Elizabeth Bishop: Life and the Memory of It* by Brett C. Millier (Berkeley, CA: University of California Press, 1993), 65. **6** William Benton, ed., *Exchanging Hats: Paintings / Elizabeth Bishop* (New York: Farrar, Straus and Giroux, 1996), 51.

a small foot, the butterflies and bottlecaps, and the throng of cheaply reproduced paper angels, some buried in sand, powerfully convey the absence of a child. And it does not matter that the images of the angels are sentimental; there is still an overriding quality of simplicity in the collage that links it to the work of Cornell. As Jonas Mekas says, speaking of Cornell's movies, there is nothing of global import to be found in them. Instead, his images are simple: "Old people in the parks. A tree full of birds. A girl in a blue dress, looking around, in the street, with plenty of time on her hands. Water dripping into the fountain ring. An angel in the cemeteries, sweetest face, under a tree. A cloud passes over the wing of the angel. What an image."[7]

The *Anjinhos* collage was one that Elizabeth Spires, in the process of interviewing Bishop in 1978, noticed in the hallway of the poet's Lewis Wharf home. Spires thought it had been made by Joseph Cornell, but Bishop told her it was "one of my little works.... It's called *Anjinhos,* which means 'little angels'. That's what they call the babies and small children who die [in Brazil]." In the interview, Bishop goes on to explain that while she was making the collage, she had visitors come to her house. She didn't think to tell them what she was doing: "When they left, I thought, My God, they must think I'm a witch or something!"[8]

As with her collage, Bishop's poetry is sharpened by the things that are seen and held, even if (or maybe especially

---

**7** Jonas Mekas, "The Invisible Cathedrals of Joseph Cornell," in *A Joseph Cornell Album* by Dore Ashton (New York: Da Capo Press, 1974), 164.
**8** Bishop, "The Art of Poetry," 285.

if) they are seen and held in memory. But she went beyond a mere facility with the visual, and indeed, the sensual, in her poetry. It is almost as if she needed to rearrange the world imaginatively in order to understand it. No wonder collage interested her—poetry is a similar art form. In Bishop's hands, it was the art of hoarding, selecting, and displaying what others might have regarded as inconsequential. She combined pieces of detritus, reshaping them to reveal unity and meaning, without losing sight of what was richly haphazard about them. As Jonas Mekas says about Cornell's collage-making, the artist was able to "transform reality by choosing, by picking out only those details which correspond to some subtle inner movement or vision, or dream."[9]

So, too, with Bishop, though her outlandish dream landscape may have been a burden at times, one that could be endlessly, tediously prolific. In "Crusoe in England," she writes:

> Dreams were the worst. Of course I dreamed of food
> and love.... But then I'd dream of things
> like slitting a baby's throat, mistaking it
> for a baby goat. I'd have nightmares of other islands
> stretching away from mine, infinities
> of islands, islands spawning islands[10]

The same juxtaposition, of distant, fantastical dreams contrasted with terrifying ones, can be seen in "Faustina, or Rock Roses," in a poem that reveals black servitude set

---

**9** Mekas, ibid, 164. **10** Bishop, "Crusoe in England," in *The Complete Poems, 1927–1979*, 165.

against white mastery: "the very worst, / unimaginable nightmare ..."[11] Whatever dreams might have brought Bishop, they seem to have been critical to her art.

Among Bishop's sketches, a magical little watercolour came to light after her death, the yellowed paper stained with two soft, watery blots. Scrawled at the bottom are the words, "E. Bishop's Patented Slot Machine." Like the *Anjinhos* collage, it is undated. It is a sketch, little more than a doodle, of what might be an old-fashioned pinball machine, standing on rickety legs, and decorated in yellow or gold along the top, with an arched sign, like a shopping-bag handle, that simply reads, "The 'Dream'." The machine itself could be housed in a glass cabinet, since we can see into it. A person operating the dream machine would apparently stand in front and use a handle to make it work. The function of the handle is unclear, though there are lines leading to a coil, not unlike the filaments of tungsten inside an incandescent light bulb. A dotted line with an arrow points to a reddish lightning bolt. "Spark," it says. The spark makes a connection with a ball shaped like an eye at the back of the machine: "Crystal Ball." The crystal ball is inserted between two structures, one like an upside-down wedding cake above, with another wedding cake below. These are numbered: 2 3 8 10 7 1 and 3 2 5 4 1.[12]

How strange is this sketch, and how reminiscent of Joseph Cornell's *Medici Slot Machine* (1942), with its image of the *Portrait of a Young Prince of the Este Family* (originally

---

**11** Bishop, ibid, 73–74. **12** Benton, ed., *Exchanging Hats: Paintings/Elizabeth Bishop*, 77.

Lace curtains at kitchen
window – E.B. House

thought to be by G.B. Moroni, but now thought to have been painted by Sofonisba Anguissola.) It contains fragments of a map of the ancient imperial palace in Rome, with a compass below, a spiral, children's jacks, and recurring images of faces.[13] Of this collage, Bishop said, "[When] I first saw the *Medici Slot Machine*.... Oh, I loved it."[14]

The poet Marianne Moore, a friend of Bishop's, became a correspondent of Cornell's, and she supported him when he applied for a Guggenheim grant in 1945. In its "sense of design...[and] consistent rigor of selection," she commented, his work constituted "poetry."[15] And it was Bishop herself who translated Octavio Paz's "Objects and Apparitions," a poem written for Joseph Cornell, whose work opened the portals of the mysterious for both writer and translator. The poem ends with an invocation to the artist: "Joseph Cornell: inside your boxes / my words become visible for a moment."[16] It is as if Paz's Spanish, turned into Bishop's English, carries her own longings.

For Bishop, as for Cornell, art allowed her to play a game in which her imagination could move freely, though there were rules by which to abide. But in Bishop's poetry, both time and space appear to be shards or fragments of a reality that once might have been intact: "Days and Distance disarrayed again / and gone."[17] Her poetry seems to be a painstaking attempt—at once visual, aural, tactile—to put these fragments back together. Things do not fit as they

---

**13** Dore Ashton, *A Joseph Cornell Album*, 222. **14** Bishop, "The Art of Poetry," 285. **15** Marianne Moore, in Dore Ashton, *A Joseph Cornell Album*, 87. **16** Octavio Paz, trans. Elizabeth Bishop, in *The Complete Poems, 1927–1979*, 276. **17** Bishop, "Argument," in *The Complete Poems, 1927–1979*, 81.

might be expected to fit, but this process, while arduous, is still whimsical. It is this quality that makes her work seem almost childlike, since the world is equally terrifying in its horrors as it is surprising in its delights.

Nowhere is this clearer to me than in her poem "12 O'Clock News," included in her collection *Geography III*, published in 1976. Some of her best-known poems are published in that collection, such as "In the Waiting Room," "The Moose," and "One Art." But it was "12 O'Clock News" that interested me, when I first read it, partly because of the poet Paul Muldoon's essay about it in his book of Oxford lectures, *The End of the Poem*. He discusses how it bridges the divide between poetry and prose, so he is attentive to the way the poem is laid out on the page. While Brett Millier, a Bishop biographer, calls this poem "more clever than profound," it is unusual in its form, in the sense of its very visual shape.[18] There is a quality of play about it, but it finds only desolation, not delight, in the world's war games; perhaps because of its resigned, ironical tone James Merrill called this Bishop's "saddest poem."[19]

When I first came upon this poem I found myself wondering what I was reading. Was it really a poem? Could it be notes for a poem? I read it again. I discovered that the "marginalia" isn't marginalia at all. It's a sort of legend for the poem. The gooseneck lamp, typewriter, and other objects listed in the left-hand column do not seem to have much to do with the news reports of the main column,

---

**18** Brett C. Millier, *Elizabeth Bishop: Life and the Memory of It*, 526.

**19** James Merrill in *The End of the Poem: Oxford Lectures*, by Paul Muldoon (New York: Farrar, Straus and Giroux), 105.

whose paragraphs take up two thirds of the remaining page. Slowly, it began to dawn on me that I was reading about the landscape of a desk, and that this landscape had become that of a war-torn country.

It makes sense that the desk has become the staging place for events occurring on a miniature scale. The locale of this world made small is ingenious since the speaker can observe it at a remove. She is a god-like journalist, one who is making reports on a war-torn nation, though the war-torn nation is a tiny principality. From her vantage point, as she looms above it, the speaker is able to make observations that occasionally have an arch, knowing tone: "At last! One of the elusive natives has been spotted!"[20] Bishop is leading us through a game, but at times the poem sounds oddly prescient, as if she is describing events in the first decade of the twenty-first century:

> The natural resources of the country being far from completely known to us, there is the possibility that this may be, or may contain, some powerful and terrifying "secret weapon."[21]

Having begun the poem when she was at Vassar, Bishop wasn't pointing to specific events: "it had nothing to do with Viet Nam or any particular war when I first wrote it, it was just fantasy."[22] It's a fantasy that is whimsical

---

**20** Bishop, "12 O'Clock News," in *The Complete Poems, 1927–1979*, 175. **21** Ibid, 175. **22** Bishop, "'The Work!': A Conversation with Elizabeth Bishop," an interview with George Starbuck in *Ploughshares: The Literary Journal at Emerson College* (1977, rpt. Boston, MA: Emerson College, 2008), 11–30.

and realistic—all the more plausible because of contrast between the two. The lighthearted tone gives way to irony and disillusion. Of the "bodies" in the dugout, which are, we know, merely cigarette butts, she reports:

> [...]They are in hideously contorted positions, all dead. We can make out at least eight bodies. These uniforms were designed to be used in guerilla warfare on the country's one snow-covered mountain peak. The fact that these poor soldiers are wearing them *here*, on the plain, gives further proof, if proof were necessary, either of the childishness and hopeless impracticality of this inscrutable people, our opponents, or of the sad corruption of their leaders.[23]

Complex play has multiple layers. It has a literal, surface level, but at a deeper level, it can parallel the larger world. In "12 O'Clock News," as in Jonathan Swift's *Gulliver's Travels*, the description of a miniature race of people might be regarded as merely colourful until we recognize ourselves.

Swift reveals the smallness of temperament of the Lilliputian emperor and his ministers, like Bishop's observation about those who rule her desktop principality. For instance, Gulliver manages to capture the entire Blefuscudian fleet, which he presents to the Emperor of Lilliput. He is not thanked for his labours, and instead, as Gulliver says: "so unmeasurable is the ambition of princes, that [His Majesty] seemed to think of nothing less than reducing the

---

**23** Bishop, "12 O'Clock News," in *The Complete Poems, 1927–1979*, 175.

whole empire of Blefuscu into a province, and governing it by a viceroy … by which he would remain sole monarch of the whole world."[24] Both Swift and Bishop reflect our own world back to us through the fantastical ones they create. Bishop pays attention to the way we view others—writing itself becomes problematic, as does the role of the writer. Who is the poet but a sadly corrupt leader, one who is responsible for the state of an embattled country?

⟨•⟩

After writing for several hours, I went upstairs to lie down for a nap. It was late morning, but I'd gotten up early that day. I took the pillow from the front bedroom where I'd been sleeping, and went into the small, turquoise room, with its sloped wall (it lay under the roof). Cut neatly into this sloped wall was an old skylight, with panes of glass that didn't quite fit. I could hear the sound of motorcycles arriving at the gas station across the road: it was a warm Sunday, and later, in the afternoon, when I went out for a walk, I discovered that the road from Great Village to Parrsboro was well travelled by Sunday bikers. I counted twenty-five or more of them, riding in clusters of two or three.

The sunlight poured through the skylight. There was an old-fashioned quilt on the bed, the kind made in my grandmother's time: it was white, decorated with bezels of

---

**24** Jonathan Swift, *Gulliver's Travels, Part I*, in *The Norton Anthology of English Literature*, 3rd Edition, eds. M. H. Abrams et al. (New York: W. W. Norton & Co. 1975), 971.

bright reds and yellows. A chamber pot was on the floor, tucked under the bed. The little room was a perfect place for a child, with its built-in wardrobe and drawers, all tidily constructed. I lay on the bed, looking up at the skylight, which had been nailed shut at one time. I wondered, idly, why there was a child's pair of scissors stuck into the long-tailed latch, keeping it from being moved. The scissors were the kind I'd once used in elementary school. Who had put them there?

I couldn't nap—the motorcycles were too loud. I got up to investigate the pair of scissors, which meant I also had to look, again, at the photographs of Elizabeth Bishop that hung on the walls. Here she was as a bright-eyed, pert-nosed child, exuding excitement, and here, as an older, more withdrawn child, and here, as a woman reclining in a chair on the patio at Samambaia, Brazil, stroking a black and white cat. This was the room in which that small squirrel child, with the crookedly-cut brown hair, had slept.

Now the church bell began ringing, and it crossed my mind that it was ringing for Ascension Sunday service at the United Church just across the road. It wasn't a recording of a bell; it was a real bell that rang out clearly in the fine spring air. I went downstairs, and from the parlour—where Bishop's cousin, a child named Frank (renamed Arthur in "First Death in Nova Scotia"), had once been laid out in a white coffin—I could see the church through the lace curtains. I moved to the kitchen, and there, through the frieze of lilac leaves beyond the window, I saw an old woman making her way to the church door, leaning heavily on her cane. This church in Great Village had once been Presbyterian, its steeple marking the village from a distance, a sharp exclamation mark, as I'd seen it on my walks along the dyke.

It had been ninety-odd years, nearly a hundred, since Elizabeth's widowed mother, Gertrude, had brought her daughter to Nova Scotia from Boston. Gertrude became more and more unstable as her time in Great Village went on, and was eventually committed, by her family, to the asylum in Dartmouth. But that summer she was still present in the house in Great Village. And one night—the night of a fire—as the speaker in "In the Village" recalls, the church bell rings as if clanging in her room, while the flames are, it seems, "burning the wallpaper beside the bed."[25] There is a commotion of voices—the grandmother issuing warnings to the grandfather, who is preparing to go and help put out the fire, and the two young aunts, called upon to restore order. Everyone is speaking at once. Someone finds a lamp; someone lights the wick. A hot, dry night; the windows of the house are open. One of the aunts goes into the small bedroom to soothe the child, while another aunt comforts the child's mother: all of them listen to the men driving the wagons on their way to fill barrels with water from the river, and then coming back with the water, cursing the horses.

When morning comes, it brings no relief. Only greyness. A single wagon rumbles over the bridge. The unravelling voices of the grandmother and aunts—something worse than the fire itself is being kept from the child. Is her mother about to scream? No, there is no scream. But everyone in the house anticipates it. And later in the day, when the

---

**25** Bishop, "In the Village," in *The Collected Prose,* 268.

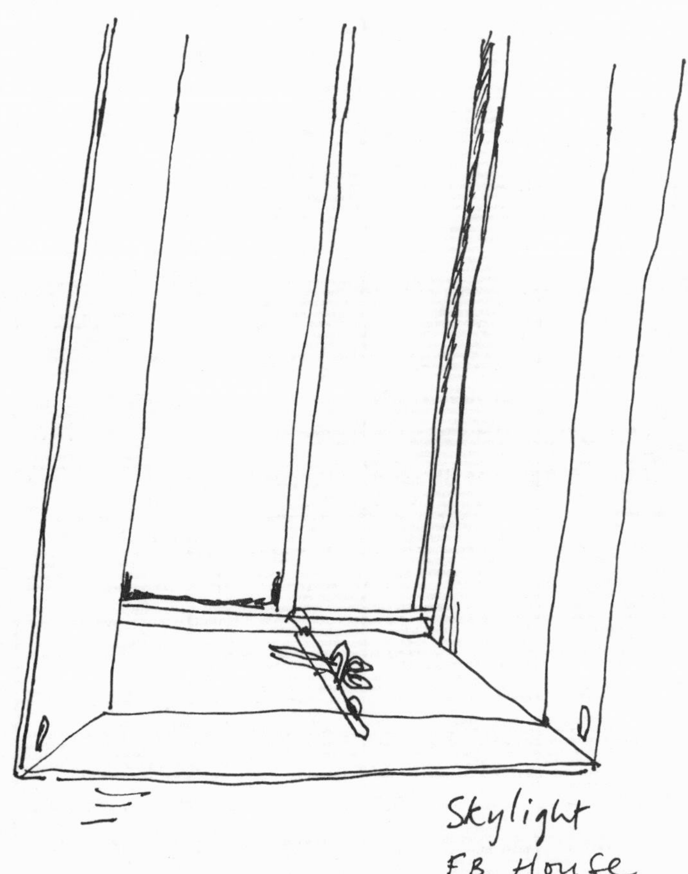
Skylight
EB House

child visits the scene of the fire, where a barn has burned, she finds the smell of the burnt hay "awful, sickening."[26]

"In the Village" is a series of vivid scenes that reveal, at an oblique angle, the story of a mother's descent into madness, and her sudden absence from a child's life. In its sharp fragmentation, with bits that are not necessarily connected, it constitutes a prose poem of great intensity. The emotional landscape is superimposed over the remembered landscape of the village. And what is offered is not the whole story, which, constructed through imagination and memory, contains bits and pieces of reality. What really happened must have been kept secret from others in the village, as it must have been kept from Bishop herself. Still, we get the sense that the warm-hearted grandparents and inquisitive, but respectful, villagers, held this small child in the same way that the school's pink map of Canada seemed to contain the whole world, rolled up, where it belonged.

When I went outside on the porch, I stood musing about this. A downy woodpecker, a female, was pecking at the trunk of the tree, its feathers—black, white, black—almost formal. It searched the trunk carefully, quaintly, sizing up the wood. At the far end of the garden, near where the blacksmith shop used to stand, was an overgrown patch of day lilies and raspberry canes, with a wooden archway through which a gardener could step.

---

**26** Ibid, 271.

Bells, hanging from a hook on the porch, tinkled softly now and then. The yellow tulips were buttery, and the rhubarb leaves, next to them, had turned into oversized oven mitts. Someone was revving an engine close by. I turned my attention to the red tulips, which were nearly gone, especially the ones along one side of the house, as were the daffodils, but the forget-me-nots were blooming, and so were the bleeding hearts, each stem hung with a row of locket-sized flowers. A ruby-throated hummingbird appeared out of nowhere, trembling in the air, with a rose-coloured gorget around its throat. It thrummed, hovering, then veered towards the crimsons and scarlets in the garden and vanished. In the thick green grass, in need of mowing, was a sprinkling of dandelions. There were the sounds of two trucks coming over the bridge, and afterwards, a sifting of wind through leaves. A robin's song, the scratchy cawing of crows. Bells again. The air was mild, soft; it was easy to think about writing without actually doing it.

There were times when I'd been reading a Bishop poem and wondered about her vantage point as she brought it into being. Maybe imagination allowed her to look on the world as a cabinet, one that she could open up from time to time, without diminishing her tenderness for, or her clarity about, what she observed.

"Here is my childhood," she seems to be saying, without fanfare, without sentimentality. "Here are the roads and houses and bridges. Let me tell you a few things that happened there." I saw her smaller self hanging over the iron bridge, gazing at the trout that once flickered through it, nearly transparent in the whisky-coloured water below. "Back then, it was like this …"

Monk's Head

# *Waterwords*

In late August, in Antigonish, I sometimes go swimming at Dunn's Beach, Monk's Head, or Pomquet Beach. The low, rolling waves—making the sound of a sleepy beast waking in a cave—the flecked clouds, the golden-brown sand, piled here and there with stones, claws, broken shells, bits of plastic, and the bumpy ridge of dunes, shiny with curved blades of marram grass: all this is abundance. A generosity of landscape, flung out in a bracelet of beaches across St. George's Bay. Monk's Head is still my favourite place to go, though walking east along the shore from Monk's Head Pond is difficult. The erosion of the cliffs, consisting of a combination of limestone, gypsum, and siltstone, has accelerated, and spruce trees have freewheeled downhill along with a giant's jumble of rocks. To get around all of this and make my way to a tiny arc of beach, secluded and wild, takes some footwork (and wet feet). It's best to do this at low tide.

But then there is the swimming itself, the reason for clambering over all the rocks to get to the hidden beach, no more than a nook, where the black guillemots fly like weird mechanical toys as they attempt to get airborne above the water. Immersing oneself in the cool, sometimes teeth-chatteringly cold, ocean can be a painfully slow process, until the body is loosened and lapped by waves.

Once I had a pact with a friend to study clouds all summer. Had I been thinking about writing poems? If so, nothing came of it. The clouds came and went; summer dissolved into autumn. (Maybe the cloud poems should still be written, as single lines on every page.) It's possible that the words written after that summer were scratchy with grains of sand, bleached with light, smoothed by water. Water and light had got into my thinking. In a place where ocean meets land, the wavering border reminded me of the first part of the Heart Sutra, one of the sutras, or teachings, of Buddhism:

> 'Here, Shariputra,
> form is emptiness, emptiness is form;
> emptiness is not separate from form,
> form is not separate from emptiness;
> whatever is form is emptiness,
> whatever is emptiness is form …'[1]

These words could form the tide line along the shore, marking the border of water and land. And at this point in the sutra it is as if Shariputra is being clapped awake by Avalokiteshvara, a noble, revered teacher. He is summoned, just as we are summoned: "Here, Shariputra…." Here and nowhere else. In this moment. For Shariputra, the realm of

---

1 Red Pine (Bill Porter), trans. and commentary, *The Heart Sutra: The Womb of Buddhas* (Washington, DC: Shoemaker & Hoard, 2004), unpaginated preface.

the here and now is where the lesson begins, though it opens into a realm of larger things. It could be a diagram showing scale, in the way that a tiny figure, clad in expedition gear, and situated in the lower corner of a photograph of a mountain, gives a sense of the vastness of the peak.

From this point, we traverse from form to emptiness as if we were in a light-filled world, with one feature of the landscape giving way to the other: "form is emptiness. . . ." We have to think about form as emptiness, as if from the point of view of form (and the things of the world that have form). But then we encounter the semi-colon hinging the sentence and arrive at the second part: "emptiness is form."

It can be difficult to think of emptiness. When I was a child, the notion of infinity was unbearable; the night sky and the moon, seen through the trees of my bedroom window, occasionally took on an ominous quality. There was no end to space.

But what is arresting about this pair of phrases—"form is emptiness; emptiness is form"—is that it shows us we can't do away with either one. Each contains the otherness that is part of it. Because we understand the validity of the sentence, we can extrapolate, extending the idea further: presence is absence; absence is presence. Loss is possession; possession is loss. A single line reveals twofold thinking: "form is emptiness; emptiness is form." This is the twofold thinking of poetry—showing us where emptiness slips into form, and where form slips into emptiness. The pressure exerted on one thing by the other reveals something to us.

What is revealed? Well, let's say I give you a line drawing of a single leaf. I've drawn it as realistically as I can: it seems almost thick and leathery, as wild oak leaves do. It looks like a narrow child's hand with knuckled-under fingers. While there has been an attempt at realism in the way it has been drawn, something is missing. It is a dream of a leaf. I've tried, and you've been gracious about it, but we both know the sketch has little to do with the leaf. The drawing is about someone trying to understand a leaf—it reveals this desire to know a leaf more than it reveals the leaf itself. In the attempt to draw the form of the leaf, I've simultaneously drawn the formlessness of the leaf. Form contains an emptiness that somehow, paradoxically, exceeds it.

Any poet worth his or her salt is aware of this sort of paradox; very good poets surprise us with it. In his poem "State of the Planet," Robert Hass reveals life in its particularities even as he gets across a sense of life's dreamy unreality. The rightness of the words reverberates:

> It's easy for us to feel that our lives are a dream—
> As this is, in a way, a dream: the flailing rain,
> The birds, the soaked red backpack of the child ...
> A dream, and we alive somewhere, somehow outside it,
> Watching.[2]

Hass is challenging us to wake up, but he's doing it in a subtle, unobtrusive way. He's not accusing us. We're simply those who watch, while the poem, and the planet, "ends with a plague." He knows we want a gentle ending, some

---

**2** Robert Hass, "State of the Planet," *Time and Materials: Poems 1997–2005* (New York: Ecco Press, 2007), 55.

lightness to offset his dark mood, but he won't give it to us. There is no restoration here, even if "the earth needs a dream of restoration— / She dances and the birds just keep on arriving, / Thousands of them, immense arctic flocks, her teeming life."[3]

But what have the teeming birds, or the child with her red backpack, to do with the next section of the Heart Sutra—"emptiness is not separate from form, / form is not separate from emptiness"? If nothing is separate, does it mean that there are no distinctions between one thing and another? Here Red Pine notes what Ching-chueh says: "According to Nagarjuna, 'Form illuminates emptiness. Without form there is no emptiness. And emptiness illuminates form. Without emptiness there is no form'."[4] One does not annihilate the other; it illuminates it. Form and emptiness can be seen as part of a web of reciprocity, each unfolding the otherness that appears to be its opposite, but which is, in fact, somehow necessary to its existence. So the notion that form is not separate from emptiness and emptiness is not separate from form becomes larger, and larger still. But as it unfolds, it remains constant.

Thich Nhat Hanh opens his commentary on the Heart Sutra with the sentence: "If you are a poet, you will see clearly that there is a cloud floating in this sheet of paper."[5] (Ah, we think, squinting to see the cloud—we are poets!) He goes on to point out how a cloud gives rain to the trees

---

**3** Ibid, 56. **4** Ching-chueh, in Red Pine, *The Heart Sutra: The Womb of Buddhas*, 81. **5** Thich Nhat Hanh, *The Heart of Understanding: Commentaries on the Prajñaparamita Heart Sutra*, ed. Peter Levitt (Berkeley, CA: Parallax Press, 1988), 3.

that allow us to have paper: it is the way he enters into a discussion of "interbeing," or the way in which all things are related, as he offers commentary on the Heart Sutra. It is not only that form is inseparable from emptiness, we realize, or that emptiness is inseparable from form, it is that things exist in relation to one another. We are woven into an ecology in which nothing exists in isolation.

Poetry reminds us of this, as it points out the relationships between one thing and another. It suggests that this *could be* that. Nor does it hold with one thing having more importance than another; it is disinclined towards relationships of power. Things have equal weight. Why shouldn't a sunflower be a clock? Why shouldn't a starfish be a child's hand? As soon as poetry has offered its gifts, it retreats. It empties its pockets, divesting itself of whistles and string, ragged ends of stories, pennies, snatches of song, crumpled bits of paper. Its irresistibility lies in all that it fails to tell us, all that it will not say. Instead, it points to an old shoe without a heel, a crack in a windowpane, a dilapidated house from which a family has departed. As Jan Zwicky says, "The emptiness of things—their inconsequence. We sense this most deeply when we sense the fullness of the world's resonance in the thing. Nothing can echo with being unless it is emptied of itself."[6] This emptiness is the ground—or groundlessness—of poetry.

A few years ago a friend of mine, John Berridge, who once taught at St. Francis Xavier University, had an exhibit

---

**6** Jan Zwicky, *Wisdom & Metaphor* (Kentville, NS: Gaspereau Press, 2003), Left 101.

of photographs at the art gallery on campus. Among the portraits of people, some of them haunting, others exuberant, were a few abstract photographs. John explained later that these abstracts were actually photographs of coloured glass. But they were more than photographs of coloured glass: they were radiant bursts of red and orange, crisp layers of blue, bubblings of gold. About a year ago, I tried to write a sequence of poems based on these photographs and some others that John subsequently produced. I tried and failed. I couldn't capture the sense of the ephemeral that would have given them poignancy. I put the poems aside. Then I put the photographs aside.

Recently, I tried again to write the sequence. This time I began with a desire to inhabit emptiness. I wanted to imagine a time before words, before form. If the words themselves were to arise out of formlessness, this had to be shown in the shape of the poetry. As I went further, I had to give up metaphor and simile. Soon I was left with bits of language, bare and exposed, but out of these I attempted to make a "formed" formlessness, without sentences or punctuation of any kind, but with certain repetitions that allowed me to move forward. Each element I introduced had to be taken away in the next breath. It was a making as well as an unmaking. What John's photographs showed me was a series of imagined landscapes in which everything was in the process of being formed. I began to envision a world arising out of the silvers and blues and crimsons of his photographs. Hidden within them were the rise and fall of mountain ranges, tumultuous oceans and skies heavy with weather. The photographs depicted form and formlessness at the same time.

⊰•⊱

There is more to the Heart Sutra, the Dalai Lama says, than an understanding of form and emptiness. Such understanding requires obligation, he observes, putting emphasis on the notion that we're inextricably linked to one another. What is required of us, if we want to put the Heart Sutra into practice, he says, is "a deep sense of commitment that *I myself* will take up the responsibility" to alleviate suffering for others.[7]

How does he propose this? Both the Dalai Lama and Thich Nhat Hanh say that what is necessary is *bodhichitta*, or compassion. Thich Nhat Hanh discusses the predicament of a prostitute, a child of fourteen or fifteen, living in Manila. He talks about her situation with grave tenderness, able to see into the poverty that reduced her to these circumstances while at the same time examining the corruption of those who have exploited her.

I read these words and remembered visiting Thailand several years before, with members of the Coady International Institute at St. Francis Xavier University. We were there for a forum highlighting citizen-driven community development, since a book was in the process of being

---

**7** Tenzin Gyatso, The Fourteenth Dalai Lama, *Essence of the Heart Sutra: the Dalai Lama's Heart of Wisdom Teachings*, trans. and ed. Geshe Thupten Jinpa (Boston: Wisdom Publications, 2005), 140.

Soft rock (gypsum)
at water's edge .. Monk's Head

written about case studies in communities around the world where such grassroots development had been possible. I had been invited along because I was helping to edit the book. And since a number of those invited to the forum were coming from cities in southeast Asia and Africa, we met in Thailand, in the coastal city of Pattaya, near Bangkok. It so happens that prostitution is endemic there. Wherever we went in the city, we saw teenagers tottering on high heels: exquisite, fine-boned girls dressed in flamboyant clothes.

One evening, under the harsh lighting of a mall, I saw a fresh-faced blond boy who could have been a Canadian, perhaps on vacation from university. He might have been in his late teens, and he was walking with a girl of no more than twelve or thirteen. They were not walking together, but the aisles were narrow. He was ahead and she was behind. Were they hand-in-hand, or was he pulling her gently behind him, towing her as if she were a small rowboat?

The doors of the mall opened out onto the wide boulevard lined with palm trees, and the beach beyond, littered with plastic, bottle tops, paper. It was evening. The sun was going down in a haze of brilliance, and the clouds, scattered across the rose and gold, were like an artist's deft markings of charcoal. I moved towards the door with a sense of foreboding, thinking of the boy, who was the age of my son, and the girl, who was hardly more than a child. And I knew that I could have written about these two, from their vastly different points of view: the boy who might have forgotten about her in a week, and the girl, who might have fallen for him, lacking the cynicism that would, no doubt, come with time.

When Thich Nhat Hanh talks about the child prostitute in Manila, he asks us to think of her locked into a situation of powerlessness: "if we look into ourselves and see her, we bear her pain, and the pain of the whole world."[8] It isn't just a case of seeing her, Thich Nhat Hanh points out, but of sensing her suffering. In fact, I could be the prostitute. Or you could be the prostitute. And here I am, or you are, in Robert Hass's poem "Ezra Pound's Proposition," in which a fourteen-year-old girl in Bangkok is chatting up a man who is passing. The way it works (beauty, sexuality, fertility, and economics), Hass says, is like this:

The World Bank arranges the credit and the dam
Floods three hundred villages, and the villagers find their way
To the city where their daughters melt into the teeming streets ...[9]

He shows how we bear responsibility for this situation: we are accountable for the credit that makes the dam possible, and so, at the same time, we are accountable for the child prostitute, with the light falling across her face, across "her lovely skin," just as we are accountable for the man outside the hotel with whom she is flirting.

It is not just that poetry asks us difficult questions. It is that poetry asks us to imagine what we think we are not, and to translate what we think we are not. We could not make such a leap without intuiting that it must be made, that writing counts upon it—and this leap is imaginative, since things have to be sensed as if they were happening here

---

**8** Thich Nhat Hanh, 38. **9** Hass, 81.

and now, conveyed by a speaker with whom we feel some sympathy. Poetry can be written from the point of view of a stump, but we have to sense what it is to be a stump. It can give us the point of view of a lemon, a spider, an icicle. A horse, a house, a blade of grass. And this is true not only of poetry, but also of fiction. How else can a sense of connection be made palpable? The truly imaginative stance, Don Domanski says, is the one in which "we realize that the entire universe stands where we are standing right now, every stone, cricket, and star occupying the same moment with us, sharing the same presence that we identify with the self ... interchangeable with the other."[10]

⁂

On a clear evening in September, a group of us gathered at an old house, one that had once been owned by a sea captain, in Bayfield, Antigonish County. Our hosts, who were renting the house for a year, took us upstairs to a widow's walk, where we stepped out into the crackling bonfire of a sunset. It was as though we had stepped onto a ledge in the air, into the blazing light: at such a time and place, we should have been able to recite a Shakespearean sonnet or two. The land behind the house, shaped like a hump-backed whale, slipped out into St. George's Bay. We were suspended, or so it seemed, above Adirondack chairs arranged in

---

**10** Don Domanski, "Afterword: Flying over Language," in *Earthly Pages: The Poetry of Don Domanski*, selected with an introduction by Brian Bartlett (Waterloo, ON: Wilfred Laurier University Press, 2007), 58.

a homey circle on the grass below. This tamed land, which became wilder beyond the border of shorn grass, unrolled into a woodlot with pockets of dense, old-growth Acadian forest—land that sloped into the spreading dark of the ocean and rose up into the frosted ridges and valleys of Cape Breton, and the remotely distant, cold stars. For those few moments, I know we talked, but I have no idea what we talked about; I was struck hard, as if I'd been walloped, by what was all around me. It was the sense of being utterly one with all that lay around us.

I glanced at the woman next to me. Could she hear the snapping light?

We turned to go inside, down the stairs to the party, talking as we went.

This is what poetry wants, what it can't get enough of. It is the sense of being connected not only with earth, water, sky, but also being profoundly at home in the world. Rainer Maria Rilke says this:

> I was standing at night on the wonderful bridge of Toledo when a star, falling through cosmic space in a tensed slow arc, simultaneously (how should I say this?) fell through my inner space: the body's dividing outline was no longer there …[11]

This is the gift, the grail, the scroll of mysteries in an ancient tongue—that shows us what it is to be, for an instant, the space in which a star is falling.

---

**11** Rainer Maria Rilke, "Notes" in *The Selected Poetry of Rainer Maria Rilke*, ed. and trans. by Stephen Mitchell (New York: Vintage International, 1989), 314–315.

It is also the moment that can't last. If Rilke knew what it was to inhabit this space, where the outer is folded into the inner, he also knew exile, as one who was constantly a stranger to himself, as well as being estranged in the world. If anything, this is what we find again and again in his poetry, as he is

> Exposed on the cliffs of the heart. Look, how tiny down there,
> look: the last village of words and, higher,
> (but how tiny) still one last
> farmhouse of feeling.[12]

This is the flip side of Rilke's ecstasy. We are back in the territory of Levinas's *il y a*, where there is no cessation of exposure: there is no shelter, there may never be shelter. It is here, on the bare cliffs, where it becomes impossible to move. Such fixity is horrifying.

Envisioning—seeing what is possible—is what imagination allows us. It provides us with a bridge from self to other, because we see into the lives of others. Without this capacity, we can't empathize, since, in such a state of fixity, we have no ability to move *towards*. We forfeit a sense of reciprocity, perhaps without even knowing that we're forfeiting it. After 9/11, the novelist Ian McEwan commented that terrorism does not have the capacity to imagine, for that would mean imagining the lives of others. Of the terrorists who flew planes into the towers of the World Trade Center,

---

**12** Rilke, "Exposed on the cliffs of the heart," 143.

McEwan stresses that "amongst their crimes, is, was, a failure of the imagination, of the moral imagination."[13]

Thinking of this, I went into my closet to ferret out some newspapers I'd kept from September 2001. They had yellowed. There was a large photograph of the expressionless face of George W. Bush. And one of Queen Elizabeth, revealing her ashen-faced shock. Faces of terror: a young man howling, a woman covering her face with her hands. Someone has picked up someone else in order to carry her to safety. One man, on a Manhattan street, with dust and debris all around him, has calmly picked up a sheet of paper in order to read it.

Another, one that I've seen repeatedly in my imagination since the time I first saw it in the newspaper, is that of people standing at the windows, now broken, of the ninetieth floor of one of the towers. They are wearing summer clothing, or maybe they've taken off their suit jackets because of the intolerable heat and lack of oxygen within the building. They look like us. It is difficult to make out the details, since they are at a distance from the photographer, but their panic seems clear. No one could get to them, and this is what disturbed me so much. Some of them look as if they are about to jump—and many probably did jump in the ensuing moments.

The single most compelling photograph, one to which I kept returning, surrounded as I was by the newspapers, was that of a violinist who was playing during a service in

---

**13** Ian McEwan was interviewed by Helen Whitney for *Frontline*, PBS (April, 2002).

Christchurch Cathedral in Vancouver. I wanted to know what piece she was playing, but the caption does not offer much information. It is clear, though, that the violinist had no idea anyone was taking her photograph, or if she did, she was oblivious. Her eyes are closed as she plays. Tears gleam on her face.

Here is someone with the capacity to imagine, to step beyond herself into the sorrow of that time. If we don't try to see the other, we're condemned to being locked into ourselves. And it seems to be what Levinas is getting at when he says, "at the very moment when my power to kill realizes itself, the Other has escaped me."[14] If we can kill, we don't have a sense of the humanity of someone else—of anyone else. So the ability to empathize is necessary if we don't want to become so hunkered down in ourselves that we might be capable of killing. More importantly, we need to empathize to participate fully in a community, and be able to give to, and take from, each other.

It was the issue of empathy that interested Edith Stein, who was a doctoral student under the philosopher Edmund Husserl. She later edited his papers, preparing them for publication (a task which Martin Heidegger, another of the protegés, also undertook). A Prussian Jew who converted to Catholicism against her family's wishes, and who later became a Carmelite nun, Stein was executed, together with her sister, in the gas chambers of Birkenau on August 9,

---

**14** Emmanuel Levinas, "Is Ontology Fundamental?" in *Basic Philosophical Writings* (*Studies in Continental Thought*) eds. Adriann Peperzak, Simon Critchley, and Robert Benasconi (Bloomington, IN: Indiana University Press, 1996), 9.

1942. Yet the brilliance of her thinking is less well known to us now than her conversion to Catholicism, her capture and death, and her subsequent, and controversial, canonization as a saint in 1998.

Stein's phenomenology takes other people into account in a radical way. She shows that empathy is not just one of the ways of sensing the world: experiencing others (or, in the parlance of phenomenologists, "constituting" others) is necessary to experiencing, or constituting, oneself. In this way, she demonstrates the importance of empathy, which not only links us to others, but shows us to be distinct:

> In fact, intersubjectivity, as brought to full consciousness in the act of empathy, reveals who we are and who we are not, what I know and what I do not know. I know that I am not the other ... however, I share with the other ...[15]

So empathy is necessary to any thinking about identity. And each of us, it turns out, is divided within: this is what enables us to empathize. In Stein's fourfold view of the individual, some aspects can be shared, such as sentience and intelligence, while some can't be shared, such as physicality and personality. For instance, no one else can feel my pain, and no one else can truly appreciate the importance of Antonin Dvořák for me. Because some aspects can't be shared, the individual remains an individual, one who is autonomous and unique, but because he or she is also able to share,

---

**15** Antonio Calcagno, *The Philosophy of Edith Stein* (Pittsburgh, PA: Duquesne University Press, 2007), 37.

connection with others is possible. Stein's view of the person is one that is open and porous in its exchange with others. Simultaneously, the person is regarded as having many sides within one, while presenting a uniqueness that can't be duplicated.[16]

Stein points out that the "I" is not lost in its empathetic consideration of someone else; on the contrary, the "I" becomes sharply realized, quite apart from another. It is because of empathy, she says, that we can be sure of what we are not. But there's more to it: something else happens when we experience things communally. As she says,

> I feel my joy while I empathetically comprehend the others' [joy].... Now I intuitively have before me what they feel. It comes to life in my feeling, and from the 'I' and 'you' arises the 'we' as a subject of a higher level.[17]

So Stein did not let the "I" dissolve, just as she did not let the "you" dissolve, but she argued that there was a wider sense of empathy (a unity of empathy, perhaps) created in the "we." We enter into the experience of joy, or sorrow, as if we were one. Because each of the individuals within the community enter into it, though without surrendering their identities—in the sense of partaking of, and giving to, a community—they help to create its inimitable personality.

---

**16** Ibid, 37–43. **17** Edith Stein, trans. Waltraut Stein, *On the Problem of Empathy*, 3rd revised ed. (Washington, DC: ICS Publications, 1989), 17.

Entering in. Partaking of. Giving to. This is the experience of being in a community with others and enjoying its benefits. But all of us are also, in some way, responsible to community, as Stein well knew, realizing that any inhumanity on the part of society had to be countered with a deeper humanity.

This brings me back to the words of the Dalai Lama, "that *I myself* will take up the responsibility" for another.[18] In the sentence immediately following this one, he says that it is not enough simply to wish for the contentment of others. Responsibility entails generating powerful compassion, he says, but to do this "one first needs to develop a sense of intimacy and empathy with other ... beings."[19] He mentions *tong len* (a Tibetan word that means "giving and taking") as a practice that might be useful in generating compassion. In this practice, meditation consists of concentrating on someone, or more than one person, who might be suffering in some way. One "imagines" absorbing the suffering of an individual, or individuals, the Dalai Lama explains, and this is followed by imagining the well-being of this individual, or individuals.[20] In other words, compassion arises out of envisioning or imagining.

It might be said that poetry, too, is like the giving and taking of *tong len*. It absorbs the world. And it works in us by revealing the world as something that is not fixed, but dynamic; not closed, but porous, allowing the exchange between one object and another, one person and another,

---

**18** Tenzin Gyatso, 140. **19** Ibid, 140. **20** Ibid, 146.

one epoch and another. We aren't held fast by the two-pronged nature of a given metaphor: either by the sunflower, or by the clock. Instead, we flicker back and forth, and it is through this gesture of being-between that we encounter possibility. So it moves between writer and reader, between speaker and listener. It takes us into the world of otherness, and then relinquishes its hold on us so that we can return to ourselves. Beyond this, poetry shows us how metaphor works as a principle, not just within a poem, but within life: it shows us ourselves *as if* we were others. It demonstrates its logic of possibility to us.

⤛•⤜

How, precisely, does poetry do this? Though it admits to the distinctions between, say, black guillemots, cumulus clouds, rose quartz, and a ten-year-old boy on a beach, it challenges any assumptions we might have about birds, clouds, rock, and child. But it begins here, by paying attention. And in much the same way as the Heart Sutra, it moves from things-in-separateness to the question of how realms interpenetrate one another. From the question of what we know about differences, such as those between form and emptiness, it shifts to the question of what we know about similarities. For instance, it might inquire into whether we know form within emptiness. It might ask whether we know the emptiness of form. And so poetry can be seen to attend to things-in-togetherness, or the way one thing folds into another, without dissolving the individual into the multiple.

So it reveals something larger. The thinking that allows

us to hold the two-sidedness of metaphor in our minds simultaneously is the same thinking that allows us to hold two aspects of the world, or reality, in our minds as a larger whole. It is the thinking that allows me to be the fourteen-year-old prostitute, and it allows you to be the fourteen-year-old prostitute. It is what allows for our connectedness to what we are not, whether animate or inanimate, so we understand what it is to have "fallen in love outward," as the poet Robinson Jeffers has Orestes say, at the end of *The Tower Beyond Tragedy*. And whenever we have "fallen in love outward," we can see things in their spaciousness. The mantra at the end of the Heart Sutra is one that implies this sense of dreamlike vastness, as if we had been transformed into clouds passing over the earth. Buddhists tell us that it is a mantra said to heal suffering: it is also regarded as a mantra of surpassing wisdom.

The first translator of the Heart Sutra was Hsuan-tsang, who, as a young monk seeking refuge from war in Szechuan, befriended an impoverished man who was very ill: in turn, the dying man taught him the Heart Sutra. Shortly afterwards, Hsuan-tsang set out on the Silk Road on a quest to learn more about the Buddha's teachings, walking as far west as Samarkand and as far south as the Ganges, and, finally, returning to China. His journey took him sixteen years. Upon his return to China in 645, he revealed to the emperor how the Heart Sutra had protected him throughout his travels.[21] And Hsuang-tsang taught him the mantra of

---

**21** Red Pine (Bill Porter), trans. and commentary, *The Heart Sutra: The Womb of Buddhas*, 17.

the Heart Sutra, which might be thought of as its inner core: *Gate, gate, paragate, parasangate, bodhi svaha.*

The words can be translated to mean "Gone, gone, gone beyond, gone completely beyond—at last." But "gate" may be written as "gata," a past passive participle of "gam," which means both "gone" and "understood."[22] The nature of understanding might be seen as taking us into the gone, and into the gone that is entirely beyond. The mantra goes beyond words, beyond anything conveyed, into a silence that is unsayable.

The commentator Fa-tsang offers something further, though. He says that an appreciation of the word "gate" should take into account its sense of "ferrying across." The repetition of "gate," he points out, needs elucidation:

> [It] means to 'ferry oneself and also ferry others.' *Paragate* means 'the other shore,' which is the place one is ferried to. And the *san* in *parasangate* means 'together,' 'everyone ferried across together.' *Bodhi* tells us what kind of 'other shore,' namely that of enlightenment. And *svaha* means 'right now.'[23]

To ferry across. When I sit on the small crescent of sand at Monk's Head, walls of tumbled rock all around, I imagine a ferry crossing the water to Cape Breton, the blur of blue hills to the east. The word "metaphor" conveys precisely this movement to us. It is a word that originates from the

---

**22** Ibid, 157–158. **23** Fa-tsang in Red Pine (Bill Porter), trans. and commentary, *The Heart Sutra: The Womb of Buddhas,* 159.

Greek, as Don McKay reminds us—"*Meta pherein:* to carry across ... a ferry whose passage one way always brings to mind the passage back."[24] I have a feeling that metaphor gives us a glimpse of the "gone" that the mantra of the Heart Sutra reveals. But metaphor also takes us back to the place we know so well. It is here and gone and here again.

The shadows have lengthened in the late afternoon. There's no ferry to be seen, just the lapping of water against rock. I haven't travelled anywhere; I'm still sitting on the tiny arc of beach at Monk's Head. I get up, retrieving my striped beach bag, slinging it over my shoulder. Brushing away the sand, I start back to the car, thinking of my responsibilities at home: dinner to help prepare, dogs to feed. But it is as if I hear the ringing of the first line of the Heart Sutra: "Here, Shariputra."

Here.

---

**24** Don McKay, *Vis à Vis: Fieldnotes on Poetry and Wilderness* (Kentville, NS: Gaspereau Press, 2001), 72.

## ACKNOWLEDGEMENTS

I am grateful for a grant from the Nova Scotia Department of Tourism, Culture & Heritage that allowed me the time to write this book.

I am indebted to Tim Lilburn, Don McKay, and Jan Zwicky, for facilitating the Colloquium on Nature Writing and Wilderness Thought at St. Peter's, Muenster, SK, in 1999, and to Tim Lilburn and Don McKay for leading the follow-up Conversation and Silence: A Symposium on Writing and the Natural World, in 2001. The discussions that arose during those gatherings pointed me along this particular path of ideas.

Many thanks to Peter Jackson for walking the Fairmont and helping with field observations for "A Hundred and Fifty Psalms at Twilight." This essay is for him. Thanks also to Chris Tragakis for reading and commenting on "Season of Ice." A course on the philosophy of Emmanuel Levinas, given by James Mensch at St. Francis Xavier University, was very helpful in the writing of "The Dark Side of Fiction's Moon." Sandra Barry is the generous spirit behind the Elizabeth Bishop House in Great Village. She was kind enough to read and comment on "World at Play." "Waterwords" is a response to thoughts about empathy raised by poets Vanessa Moeller and Erina Harris. This essay is for Beth Parker, who has helped me understand both *tong len* and the Heart Sutra.

To the Gaspereau gang, especially Andrew, Gary, and Kate, thank you for giving this book a home.

Loving thanks to my mother, Janet, and my sisters, Jennifer and Sue.

And, always, to Paul, David, and Sarah.

## A NOTE ON THE TYPE

The text of this book was set in a digital revival of types cut by the French printer and punchcutter, Pierre-Simon Fournier (1712–68). During his lifetime, Fournier is said to have cut over 60,000 punches for 147 alphabets of his own design. He also broke the monopoly on music printing in France and invented a standardized point system for music type. Two of Fournier's typefaces were revived by the Monotype Corporation in the 1920s. During the research and development of the Fournier revival by Monotype, the company's typographical advisor (a scholar named Stanley Morison whose relationship with the engineers at the typeworks might be characterized as strained) returned from a trip abroad to discover that the works had proceeded to cut the Fournier without him. In his opinion, the inferior of the two designs had been produced; regardless, Monotype Fournier appeared in 1925 and was put to admirable use at the Cambridge University Press and in the Nonesuch Press's seven-volume Shakespeare, completed in 1933. Morison's preferred design was later produced in a limited range and used in volume five of *The Fleuron* in 1930. This second type, named Barbou, was not released to the general trade until 1968, marking Fournier's bicentenary. No digital version of Barbou is commercially available at the present time, which demonstrates the potential historical ramifications of mixing travel and office politics. *Digital versions preserve Fournier's sharp italic, which was cut with a slightly smaller x-height than the roman. This imbalance results in an unusual shift in colour when the italic and roman are used together on the same line. Unlike present-day typographers, Fournier viewed the italic as an equal and distinct font, not as a helpmate to the roman, and he cut his italics accordingly. Fournier would no doubt be amused at the way in which present-day convention has fused his two independent type designs together.* A.S.

Text & illustrations copyright © Anne Simpson, 2009

The poem "A Woman, an Owl, a Boy" is from *Quick* by Anne Simpson, copyright © 2007. Published by McClelland & Stewart Ltd. Used with permission of the publisher.

All rights reserved. No part of this publication may be reproduced in any form without the prior written consent of the publisher. Any requests for the photocopying of any part of this book should be directed in writing to the Canadian Copyright Licensing Agency.

Gaspereau Press acknowledges the support of the Canada Council for the Arts, the Nova Scotia Department of Tourism, Culture & Heritage and the Government of Canada through the Book Publishing Industry Development Program.

Typeset in Fournier by Andrew Steeves & printed & bound at Gaspereau Press under the direction of Gary Dunfield.

3 5 7 6 4 2

*Library & Archives Canada Cataloguing in Publication*

Simpson, Anne, 1956–
The marram grass : poetry & otherness / Anne Simpson.

Includes bibliographical references.
ISBN 978-1-55447-072-3 (bound) ISBN 978-1-55447-071-6 (pbk.)

1. Poetry. 2. Creation (Literary, artistic, etc.). I. Title.
PS8587.I54533M37 2009 808.1 C2009-900218-3

GASPEREAU PRESS LIMITED
*Gary Dunfield & Andrew Steeves* ☙ *Printers & Publishers*
47 Church Avenue, Kentville, NS, Canada B4N 2M7
*www.gaspereau.com*